Karl Barth

Translated by Grover Foley

Evangelical Theology: An Introduction

WILLIAM B. EERDMANS PUBLISHING COMPANY
GRAND RAPIDS MICHIGAN

Evangelical Theology: An Introduction was translated from the German text, *Einführung in die evangelische Theologie,* published by EVZ-Verlag, Zürich.

First American edition published by Holt, Rinehart and Winston. This edition published 1979 through special arrangement with TVZ Verlag, Zürich by Wm. B. Eerdmans Publishing Co., Grand Rapids, Michigan 49503.

The first five lectures of this volume were delivered under the auspices of the Divinity School, the University of Chicago, and were "The Annie Kinkead Warfield Lectures of 1962" at the Princeton Theological Seminary.

Library of Congress Cataloging in Publication Data

Barth, Karl, 1886-1968.
  Evangelical theology.

  Translation of Einführung in die evangelische Theologie.
  "The first five lectures of this volume were delivered under the auspices of the Divinity School, the University of Chicago, and were 'The Annie Kinkead Warfield Lectures of 1962' at the Princeton Theological Seminary."
  Reprint of the 1st ed. published by Holt, Rinehart and Winston, New York.
  1. Theology, Doctrinal — Introductions. I. Title.
[BT65.B313 1979] 230 79-16735
ISBN 0-8028-1819-6

Some weeks after I had concluded in Basel the writing and delivering of these lectures—and with them my academic career—I had the opportunity of shaking the dust of Basel from my feet and boarding an airplane which carried me from there in a high arch over Germany, Scotland, Greenland, and the icy wilderness of Labrador. In but a few hours it brought me, for the first time, to Chicago, into the very heart of that altogether different land which Europeans liked earlier to call, not without justification, "the new world."

The present work, *Evangelical Theology: An Introduction*, will now appear in the United States in the English language. I delivered the first five of these lectures in Chicago and Princeton, and the first one also in Richmond and San Francisco, using an English manuscript which had been carefully prepared by Grover Foley (who likewise translated the whole book) and which was then again and again revised by my son Markus and myself.

I am happy now to be able to add a few somewhat personal words of remembrance, greetings, and thanks to the many old and new friends and brothers, both familiar and unfamiliar, whom I met during my stay in America. I was everywhere received and lodged by them in pleasant surroundings and with great hospitality, and they also heard and questioned me with great diligence and attention.

"How do you like that strange place called the United States?" This is what I was asked by a dusky theological colleague (not a Roman Catholic this time, but a literally black colleague) with a subtle smile, soon after my arrival in Chicago. Similar questions about my "impressions" of America have often been addressed to me by others (and occasionally even in public). I have always answered somewhat evasively. Even in Washington, where I had the opportunity of spending an interesting evening with a group of younger men who stood near to the President, I prudently offered only certain questions and no "statements." Most certainly, I will not write an article on "America," much less a book, for if I know one thing about America, after having spent seven weeks in that "strange place" (and then only in ten of its fifty states) and having opened my eyes and ears as widely as possible, it is certainly this: that I know all too little about America to be able to speak competently about it.

In fact, I did have "impressions," but I could actually summarize them only with the one word, "fantastic"—a word which, by the way, plays a remarkable role in one of Tennessee Williams' dramas that I saw during my stay in New York. And I would have to reproduce these impressions in similar language (if I had the spirit and means of non-objective art at my command). Yes, "fantastic" is the word for all that: the numberless streams, plains, hills, and mountains between the two oceans, and the whole landscape over which we flew in all directions or through which we hurried by automobile; the wilderness of Arizona, the Grand Canyon (where I had good reasons for refraining from making the descent), the bay of San Francisco together with the Golden Gate bridge; Chicago and New York with their gigantic buildings, with their incoming and outgoing highways filled with the continuous gleaming motion of innumerable cars, with their swarms of individuals of all lands, races, occupations, and endeavors; the strange unity as well as contrast of humanity in the East, West, and South of the continent; the thorough organization and standardization (to a certain extent competing with divine providence) of all life, including that of the

Church and even of theological science; the pertinent, but also sometimes rather impertinent, curiosity and descriptive art of the American journalist. . . ! For me it was also "fantastic" to see the thousands who streamed to my lectures and to my public discussions in Chicago and Princeton, and also to see myself suddenly engulfed by such an avalanche of "publicity," to which I was quite unaccustomed. ("Advertising helps it happen" I read in great letters on a billboard at the side of an American highway.)

While in America I experienced a few things which, although not of primary importance, were very significant to me. My little book of sermons from the Basel prison, now also translated into English, won me entrance into three great American prisons. There, along with some quite bad aspects, I saw many hopeful signs, and I had the very best impressions of the intentions of the directors and chaplains of these houses. The unforgettable hymnal greetings which I received in these places from the Church choirs, mostly composed of Negroes, were as powerful as they were impressive! Chinatown in San Francisco was also unforgettable, as was a guided stroll through the somewhat ill-famed East Harlem in the northern part of Manhattan Island. But my unquenchable historical curiosity led me also to visit a whole series, though by no means all, of the sites of the American Civil War. I had already long before acquired from afar a literary interest in its events and personalities. Now informed eagerly and precisely in detail by older and younger experts, I obtained a vivid and enduring picture of what was done, undone, and, above all, suffered by the blue "Yankees" and the gray "Rebels" under the leadership of their more or less gifted generals on the broad fields (nowadays cared for in the main quite appropriately) at Manassas-Bull Run, Fredericksburg, Chancellorsville, and, above all, Gettysburg, and the sur-

roundings of Richmond. And it was only natural that I
could not omit devoting, in front of his impressive monu-
ment in Washington, a serious "minute of silence" to
Abraham Lincoln, the greatest and, from first to last, the
decisive man in that American period of heroism and
terror. (According to a promise made to me, his complete
works are soon supposed to make this small house of
mine in Basel smaller still and my knowledge of the
American past greater still.)

Parenthetically, how does that old history, now just
a hundred years past, concern me? I could say in reply (once again somewhat evasively) that there was
once another D.D. and professor of systematic theology
whose opinion was that this history eminently concerned him. His name was R. L. Dabney, a professor in
Richmond and later in Austin, Texas who, moreover,
also left behind a work of dogmatics. During the Civil
War, Dabney was not only a chaplain but the chief of
staff of the famous Rebel General Stonewall Jackson,
who in his own right was a strict Presbyterian, a deacon
of the Church of Lexington, Virginia, and a conductor
of Sunday school and prayer hours! There are really
"more things in heaven and earth. . ."!

On the other hand, I also had the opportunity of gaining certain special impressions of the American present
in the form of all sorts of human encounters, though I
dare not construct any precise image from them. (Thou
shalt make no image, no abstraction, including none of
the American, *the* Swiss, *the* German, etc.!) For hours
or even whole evenings I sat together with businessmen,
actors, Talmud-Jews, journalists, Roman Catholic theologians, and even with a small group of real live Communists. Strangely enough I only once met with a large
group of preachers, but naturally I encountered individual professors and students of a whole series of theological faculties and seminaries. I was with Billy

Graham as well as with the conscientious and thought-
ful New York attorney William Stringfellow, who
caught my attention more than any other person; while
unfortunately my relationship to the courageous Negro
pastor Martin Luther King was confined to being photo-
graphed together in front of a church door. If, after
all of these encounters, I have anything to regret, it is
that on most such occasions, as the circumstances demanded, I was obliged to speak far too much, while I
would have preferred to ask questions, to listen, and to
learn as much as was allowed by the tempo and the very
different types of English in which I was addressed. I
actually only became silent (apart from the political
evening in Washington) in the presence of two extraordinarily significant women: Mrs. Anna M. Kross,
Commissioner of Correction of New York City, who is
involved in energetic reform of prison conditions there,
and Dr. Anna Hedgeman, the champion of a new and
self-consciously rising American Negro population,
whom I came to know in New York only shortly before
my departure. A third lady, the one immortalized in the
Statue of Liberty in the harbor of New York, seemed
to be pleased enough at my presence but still only
silently waved to me!

One reason why I have somewhat broadly described
all this here is to show the future American readers of
this book that I have had intense pleasure at being in
their land and in their midst. There are no grounds at
all for supposing that I was full of distrust upon coming to them and while lingering among them. That I believe neither in a Soviet heaven on earth, nor in a similar
Swiss or American terrestrial paradise, nor in any "way
of life" constructed by men, is another matter. The only
reason why I had not earlier visited America is that
until now I could not afford any such extensive absence
from my writing desk. Who knows, moreover, whether

in retrospect it may not appear better from both the American point of view and my own that this visit has only now taken place, and who knows whether everything would have gone so peacefully, pleasantly, and amicably if I had appeared in the United States fifteen or perhaps even thirty years ago? Whatever the case may be, I now have a much more concrete picture than before of the existence (and the foreground and background of the existence) of American Christians and their fellow men. These lectures were not written for them but for my Basel hearers. It may be that, if they had been written after, instead of before, my trip to America, one thing or another would have been said and expressed in a different way. All the same, my American readers for their part may now have gotten to know me somewhat more concretely; they may have noticed that I am neither the "prophet," the "monumental patriarch," nor the "giant of theology," as which I was here and there described, and just as little the gloomy theological gladiator and fire-eater whom many there may have had before their eyes from the times of my early commentary on *Romans* and the angry "No!" to Brunner. Instead, I may now hope that the author of this book may have become familiar to many readers, if not to all, as a normal human being who is considerably involved in all sorts of human affairs, and distinguished from other men only by the simple fact that he chiefly has devoted his days to a special emphasis on the question of proper theology and that he would be happy if others would also devote themselves in all seriousness to this question again and again. This foreword's little review of those seven weeks may appear to be a somewhat astonishing resumé, but it may serve the purpose of contributing in a small way to the understanding of the author and the book itself.

As far as I can now see, the five lectures which are

to be found at the beginning of this book have, on the whole, been received in the United States with astonishing courtesy and appreciation. When I arrived and read the words with which the *Christian Century* intended to greet me, I understood something of their dread that one or another of my hearers might suppose himself all too easily dispensed from historical criticism and other achievements of the nineteenth century. When I left I heard again a question that apparently had gone unanswered: "How shall we make the jump from Moses to Mozart, from Mesopotamia (!) to East Germany, from obedience toward Caesar to defiance of Hitler?" Another question was whether I do not mythologize the Jews of the present by considering and addressing them as identical with the people of the Old Testament. And *Christianity Today* informed me that the old uneasiness smoldering in the conservative camp has still not been extinguished concerning what I have supposedly been heard to say about the authority of the Bible and the relationship of *Geschichte* and *Historie*. I eagerly await the further echoes: whether these and similar reservations will now be further weakened or still more strengthened among readers of the rest of the lectures, and whether certain wrinkles which I could not overlook on the brows of the theological professors and students who questioned me (in spite of all the readiness with which they listened) will vanish or will grow deeper and darker. Certainly, much still remains to be clarified and explained. I only hope that all readers will take my word that I do not presume to have spoken even humanly ultimate words in those five lectures and now in these seventeeen. And by the way, I also understand the *Church Dogmatics* (which can now also be read in America), not as the conclusion, but as the initiation of a new exchange of views about the question of proper theology, the established knowledge of God, and the

obedient service of God among and for men. I think I
have seen unmistakably that a new discussion of this
question has also been undertaken in America. And I
have even a faint hope that this discussion might one
day be pursued there in a more fruitful manner than
in the waters of European theology, which are at present
somewhat stagnant. What we need on this and the other
side of the Atlantic is not Thomism, Lutheranism, Cal-
vinism, orthodoxy, religionism, existentialism, nor is
it a return to Harnack and Troeltsch (and least of all
is it "Barthianism"!), but what I somewhat cryptically
called in my little final speech at Chicago a "theology of
freedom" that looks ahead and strives forward. More or
less or something other than that would scarcely be
suitable, either here or there, to the foundation, object,
and content of evangelical theology or to the nearly
apocalyptic seriousness of our time.

KARL BARTH

FROM THE FOREWORD TO THE
GERMAN EDITION

I hope none of those who find the volumes of the *Church
Dogmatics* too thick will complain about the energetic
brevity with which I express myself here. Since I could
not very well announce "Dogmatics" as a lecture topic
for but one hour each week, I chose to use the opportunity of this swan song for another purpose. I wanted to
render a short account to myself and my contemporaries
of what, up to now, I have basically sought, learned, and

represented from among all the paths and detours in the field of evangelical theology during my five years as a student, twelve years as a preacher, and subsequent forty years as a professor. Perhaps I also had the secondary intention of offering to the present-day younger generation a survey of an alternative to the *mixophilosophicotheologia* (a word coined by Abraham Calov in days long past!)—to the mixture of philosophy and theology which, at present, seems to make such a tremendous impression upon many as the newest thing under the sun. I did not wish to do this in the form of a further *Credo,* an "Outline" of dogmatics or a comparable *Summula.* So I chose the form of an "introductory" presentation, which in all events had not appeared for some time in the program of study of our faculty at Basel.

KARL BARTH

CONTENTS

Evangelical Theology: An Introduction

Theology is one among those human undertakings tra-
ditionally described as "sciences." Not only the natural
sciences are "sciences." Humanistic sciences also seek
to apprehend a specific *object* and its environment in
the manner *directed* by the phenomenon itself; they
seek to understand it on its own terms and to speak of it
along with all the implications of its *existence*. The word
"theology" seems to signify a special science, a very
special science, whose task is to apprehend, understand,
and speak of "God."

But many things can be meant by the word "God."
For this reason, there are many kinds of theologies.
There is no man who does not have his own god or gods
as the object of his highest desire and trust, or as the
basis of his deepest loyalty and commitment. There is no
one who is not to this extent also a theologian. There is,
moreover, no religion, no philosophy, no world view that
is not dedicated to some such divinity. Every world view,
even that disclosed in the Swiss and American national
anthems, presupposes a divinity interpreted in one way
or another and worshiped to some degree, whether
wholeheartedly or superficially. There is no philosophy
that is not to some extent also theology. Not only does
this fact apply to philosophers who desire to affirm—or
who, at least, are ready to admit—that divinity, in a
positive sense, is the essence of truth and power of
some kind of highest principle; but the same truth is
valid even for thinkers denying such a divinity, for
such a denial would in practice merely consist in trans-
ferring an identical dignity and function to another
object. Such an alternative object might be "nature,"
creativity, or an unconscious and amorphous will to life.

It might also be "reason," progress, or even a redeeming nothingness into which man would be destined to disappear. Even such apparently "godless" ideologies are theologies.

The purpose of these remarks is not to introduce the world of these many theologies with their many gods. We will not compare them historically or offer critical conjectures regarding them. No position will be taken on behalf of one against all the others, nor will the others be subordinated and related to this one. There is no apparent reason why these many theologies should have anything essential in common with that which we want to discuss under the title "theology"; nor is it clear how we could fruitfully set them in relation to our task. Among themselves they have one thing in common, something that immediately casts a significant light on the gods to which they are dedicated. Each one of them considers and represents itself as the best theology because, even should it not be the only right one, it claims to be still more right than the others. From the very beginning, as the fable of the three rings suggests, we should beware of participating in this competition. In one of his plays the German poet Lessing compares the claims of the Jewish, Mohammedan, and Christian religions to the claims of three brothers. Each one of them had received a precious ring from the hands of their dying father. Each claimed to have received his father's one and only precious ring, rather than an exact copy of it. The warning contained in this fable is obvious, even if we do not choose to follow Lessing's opinion that perhaps the genuine ring was lost and nothing else but imitations were left in the brothers' hands. The best theology (not to speak of the only right one) of the highest, or even the exclusively true and real, God would have the following distinction: it would *prove* itself—and in this regard Lessing was altogether right—by the demonstration of the Spirit and of its power. However, if it should hail and proclaim *itself* as such, it would by this very fact betray that it certainly is *not* the one true theology.

For this reason we will dispense with any comparison or evaluation that would separate or synthesize various theologies. Instead, let this simple pointer suffice: the theology to be introduced here is *evangelical* theology. The qualifying attribute "evangelical" recalls both the New Testament and at the same time the Reformation of the sixteenth century. Therefore, it may be taken as a dual affirmation: the theology to be considered here is the one which, nourished by the hidden sources of the documents of Israel's history, first achieved unambiguous expression in the writings of the New Testament evangelists, apostles, and prophets; it is also, moreover, the theology newly discovered and accepted by the Reformation of the sixteenth century. The expression "evangelical," however, cannot and should not be intended and understood in a confessional, that is, in a denominational and exclusive, sense. This is forbidden first of all by the elementary fact that "evangelical" refers primarily and decisively to the Bible, which is in some way respected by all confessions. Not all so-called "Protestant" theology is evangelical theology; moreover, there is also evangelical theology in the Roman Catholic and Eastern orthodox worlds, as well as in the many later variations, including deteriorations, of the Reformation departure. What the word "evangelical" will objectively designate is that theology which treats of the *God of the Gospel*. "Evangelical" signifies the "catholic," ecumenical (not to say "conciliar") *continuity and unity* of this theology. Such theology intends to apprehend, to understand, and to speak of the God of the Gospel, in the midst of the variety of all other theologies and (without any value-judgment being implied) in distinction from them. This is the God who reveals himself in the Gospel, who himself speaks to men and acts among and upon them. Wherever he becomes the object of human science, both its source and its norm, there is *evangelical* theology.

Let us now attempt to describe evangelical theology. An account of its most important characteristics will serve as a prelude to clarify the uniqueness which it derives from its object. Among these characteristics there is none that, *mutatis mutandis*, presupposing the requisite changes, could not and would not have to be the characteristic of other sciences as well. Although we will not expand upon this observation here, we will indicate the extent to which these general characteristics are specific characteristics of *theological* science.

In the first place, it was not Lessing who originally forbade evangelical theology to award itself the prize in comparison with other theologies or, what is more, to pass itself off in any one of its forms as divine wisdom and doctrine. For the very reason that it is devoted to the God who proclaims himself in the Gospel, evangelical theology cannot claim for itself that authority which belongs to him alone. The God of the Gospel is the God who mercifully dedicates and delivers himself to the life of all men—including their theologies. Nevertheless, he *transcends* not only the undertakings of all other men but also the enterprise of evangelical theologians. He is the God who again and again discloses himself anew and must be discovered anew, the God over whom theology neither has nor receives sovereignty. The separation and distinction of this one true God from all the others can only be continually his own deed. This deed cannot be reduplicated by any human science, not even by a theology which is dedicated explicitly to him alone. Even in this basic consideration he is, without doubt, a God wholly different from other gods. Other gods do not seem to prohibit their theologies from boasting that each one is the most correct or even the only correct theology. On the contrary, such gods even seem to urge their respective theologians to engage in such boasting. Evangelical theology, on the other hand, no doubt can and should base its thought and speech on the decision and deed by which God lets his honor pale all other gods; however, it would definitely *not* think and speak about such acts if, by this, it wished to win renown for itself according to the example of other theologies. For better or for worse, it must set forth and proceed along its own way, a way which is fundamentally and totally different from that of other theologies. All the same, evangelical theology must not lose patience when it is viewed and understood in the same categories as those others. It must even tolerate being compared and seen in relationship to them under the rubric "philosophy of religion" (though let me warn you that, for its part, it cannot join in this attempt). It can expect justice for itself only by the fact that God justifies it. It can give only him and not itself the glory. Evangelical theology is *modest* theology, because it is determined to be so by its object, that is, by him who is its subject.

In the second place, there are three subordinate presuppositions with which evangelical theology works. The first is the general event of human *existence* in its insoluble dialectic, which theology sees confronted by the self-proclamation of God in the Gospel. Secondly, there is the particular *faith* of those men who not only are allowed but are also ready and willing to acknowledge God's self-proclamation. They know and confess for all people and specifically for his chosen witnesses that God authenticates himself. Thirdly, there is the general and the particular presupposition of *reason*, the capacity for perception, judgment, and language common to believers as well as to all men. It is this capacity that makes it technically possible for them to participate actively in the theological pursuit of knowledge, an endeavor directed to the God who proclaims himself in the Gospel. However, this does not mean that theology would be ordered, much less even allowed, to choose for its object and theme—in place of God—human existence or faith or man's spiritual capacity (even if this should include a special religious capacity, a "religious a priori"). Such topics—if made dominant—would render homage to theology's unique theme only subsequently and incidentally. They could not avoid also arousing the suspicion that "God" might be, after all, only a mode of speaking, comparable to the symbolic role of the King of England. Theology is well aware that the God of the Gospel has a genuine interest in human existence and, in fact, awakens and calls man to faith in him; it knows that in this way God claims and arouses man's entire spiritual capacity, more, in fact, than his spiritual capacity. But theology is interested in all this because it is primarily and comprehensively interested in God himself. The dominant presupposition of its thought and speech is *God*'s own proof of his existence and sovereignty. If theology wished to reverse this relationship, and instead of relating man to *God,* related God to *man,* then it would surrender itself to a new Babylonian captivity. It would become the prisoner of some sort of anthropology or ontology that is an underlying interpretation of existence, of faith, or of man's spiritual capacity. Evangelical theology is neither compelled nor commissioned to embrace such an undertaking. It bides its time and confidently lets things take their course, whatever the way in which existence, faith, the spiritual capacity of man, his selfhood, and self-understanding may present themselves in confrontation with the God of the Gospel who precedes them all. With respect to those subordinate presuppositions, theology is, for all its modesty, in an exemplary way a *free* science. This means it is a science which joyfully respects the mystery of the freedom of its object and which, in turn, is again and again freed by its object from any dependence on subordinate presuppositions.

In the third place, the object of evangelical theology is God in the *history* of his *deeds*. In this history he makes himself *known*. But in it he also *is* who he is. In it he has and proves, in a unity which precludes the precedence of one over the other, both his existence and his essence. The God of the Gospel, therefore, is neither a thing, an item, an object like others, nor an idea, a principle, a truth, or a sum of truths. God can be called the truth only when "truth" is understood in the sense of the Greek word *aletheia*. God's being, or truth, is the event of his self-disclosure, his radiance as the Lord of all lords, the hallowing of his name, the coming of his kingdom, the fulfillment of his will in all his work. The sum of the truths about God is to be found in a sequence of events, even in all the events of his being glorious in his work. These events, although they are distinct from one another, must not be bracketed and considered in isolation.

Let it be noted that evangelical theology should neither repeat, re-enact, nor anticipate the history in which God is what he is. Theology cannot make out of this history a work of its own to be set in motion by itself. Theology must, of course, give an account of this history by presenting and discussing human perceptions, concepts, and formulations of human language. But it does this appropriately only when it *follows* the living God in those unfolding historical events in which he is God. Therefore, in its perception, meditation, and discussion, theology must have the character of a living *procession*. Evangelical theology would forfeit its object, it would belie and negate itself, if it wished to view, to understand, and to describe any one moment of the divine procession in "splendid isolation" from others. Instead, theology must describe the dynamic interrelationships which make this procession comparable to a bird in flight, in contrast to a caged bird. Theology would forfeit its object if it should cease to recount the "mighty works of God," if it should transfer its interest instead to the examination of a material God or merely godly matters. Regardless of what the gods of other theologies may do, the God of the Gospel rejects any connection with a theology that has become paralyzed and static. Evangelical theology can only exist and remain in vigorous motion when its eyes are fixed on the God of the Gospel. Again and again it must distinguish between what God made happen and will make happen, between the old and the new, without despising the one or fearing the other. It must clearly discern the yesterday, today, and tomorrow of its own presence and action, without losing sight of the unity. It is just from this point of view that evangelical theology is an eminently *critical* science, for it is continually exposed to judgment and never relieved of the crisis in which it is placed by its object, or, rather to say, by its living subject.

In the fourth place, the God of the Gospel is no lonely God, self-sufficient and self-contained. He is no "absolute" God (in the original sense of absolute, i.e., being detached from everything that is not himself). To be sure, he has no equal beside himself, since an equal would no doubt limit, influence, and determine him. On the other hand, he is not imprisoned by his own majesty, as though he were bound to be no more than the personal (or impersonal) "wholly other." By definition, the God of Schleiermacher cannot show mercy. The God of the Gospel can and does. Just as his oneness consists in the unity of his life as Father, Son, and Holy Spirit, so in relation to the reality distinct from him he is free *de jure* and *de facto* to be the God of *man*. He exists neither *next to* man nor merely *above* him, but rather *with* him, *by* him and, most important of all, *for* him. He is *man*'s God not only as Lord but also as father, brother, friend; and this relationship implies neither a diminution nor in any way a denial, but, instead, a confirmation and display of his divine essence itself. "I dwell in the high and holy place, and also with him who is of a contrite and humble spirit, . . ." (Isaiah 57:15.) This he does in the history of his deeds. A God who confronted man simply as exalted, distant, and strange, that is, a divinity without humanity, could only be the God of a *dysangelion*, of a "bad news" instead of the "good news." He would be the God of a scornful, judging, deadly *No*. Even if he were still able to command the attention of man, he would be a God whom man would have to avoid, from whom he would have to flee if he were able to flee, whom he would rather not know, since he would not in the least be able to satisfy his demands. Such a god might be embodied in deified "progress," or even more likely by the progressive man.

Many other theologies may be concerned with such exalted, superhuman, and inhuman gods, who can only be the gods of every sort of bad news, or *dysangelion*. But the God who is the object of evangelical theology is just as lowly as he is exalted. He is exalted precisely in his lowliness. And so his inevitable No is enclosed in his primary Yes to man. In this way, what God wills for man is a helpful, healing, and uplifting work, and what he does with him brings peace and joy. Because of this he is really the God of the *euangelion*, the Evangel, the Word that is good for man because it is gracious. With its efforts, evangelical theology responds to this gracious Yes, to God's self-proclamation made in his friendliness toward man. It is concerned with God as the God of *man,* but just for this reason, also with man as *God's* man. In evangelical theology, man is absolutely not, as Nietzsche has put it, "something that must be over-come." On the contrary, for evangelical theology, man is that creature destined by God to be a conqueror. Strictly speaking, therefore, the word "theology" fails to exhaust the meaning of "evangelical theology," for one decisive dimension of the object of theology is not expressed clearly by it. This dimension is the free love of God that evokes the response of free love, his grace (*charis*) that calls for gratitude (*eucharistia*). "Theo-anthropology" would probably express better who and what is at stake here, with the provision that this should never be confused with "anthropotheology."* Let us stick, therefore, to "theology," as long as we do not forget that this theology is "evangelical" in the special sense we have just discussed. Since it is "evangelical," it can by no means be devoted to an inhuman God, for in that case it would become *legalistic* theology. Evangelical theology is concerned with Immanuel, God with us! Having this God for its object, it can be nothing else but the most thankful and *happy* science!

I would like to forgo any special explanation of the word "introduction," which appears in the title of this work. At the same time, I wish to refrain from any dis-cussion (which would be both polemic and irenic) of the manner in which a similar task has been conceived and carried out by Schleiermacher, as a "Short Presentation of Theological Study," and by various others, as a "The-ological Encyclopedia." Whether and to what extent an *introduction* to evangelical theology is offered here may become clear during the process by which I attempt to present it.

* As we previously indicated in point two on pages 7–9.

I THE PLACE OF THEOLOGY

In this and the next three lectures we will undertake to determine the special *place* of that theology, which, according to our previous explanation, desires to be evangelical theology. What concerns us is not the place, right, and possibility of theology within the domain and limits of general culture; especially not within the boundaries of the *universitas litterarum,* or what is otherwise known as general humanistic studies! Ever since the fading of its illusory splendor as a leading academic power during the Middle Ages, theology has taken too many pains to justify its own existence. It has tried too hard, especially in the nineteenth century, to secure for itself at least a small but honorable place in the throne room of general science. This attempt at self-justification has been no help to its own work. The fact is that it has made theology, to a great extent, hesitant and halfhearted; moreover, this uncertainty has earned theology no more respect for its achievements than a very modest tip of the hat. Strange to say, the surrounding world only recommenced to take notice of theology in earnest (though rather morosely) when it again undertook to consider and concentrate more strongly upon its own affairs. Theology had first to renounce all apologetics or external guarantees of its position within the environment of other sciences, for it will always stand on the firmest ground when it simply *acts* according to the law of its own being. It will follow this law without lengthy explanations and excuses. Even today, theology has by no means done this vigorously and untiringly enough. On the other hand, what are "culture" and "general science," after all? Have these concepts not become strangely unstable within the last fifty years? At any rate, are they not too beset by problems for us at present to be guided by them? All the same, we should certainly not disdain reflecting on what the rest of the academic world actually must think of theology. It is worth considering the place of theology within the university; discussion may be held about the reason and justification for locating this modest, free, critical, and happy science *sui generis* in such an environment. But for the present moment, this question may be considered secondary. Compared to it, other questions are much more pressing. Who knows whether the answer to such secondary questions might not be reserved for the third millennium, when a new light may perhaps be cast on theology and its academic *ambiance?*

The "place" of theology, as understood here, will be determined by the impetus which it receives from within its own domain and from its own *object*. Its object—the philanthropic God Himself—is the law which must be the continual starting point of theology. It is, as the military might say, the post that the theologian must take and keep, whether or not it suits him or any of his fellow creatures. The theologian has to hold this post at all costs, whether at the university or in the catacombs, if he does not wish to be imprisoned for dereliction of duty.

The word "theology" includes the concept of the *Logos*. Theology is a *logia*, logic, or language bound to the *theos*, which both makes it possible and also determines it. The inescapable meaning of logos is "word," however much Goethe's Faust felt that he could not possibly rate "the word" so highly. The Word is not the only necessary determination of the place of theology, but it is undoubtedly the first. Theology itself is a word, a human response; yet what makes it theology is not its own word or response but the Word which it hears

and to which it *responds*. Theology stands and falls with
the Word of God, for the Word of God precedes all
theological words by creating, arousing, and challenging
them. Should theology wish to be more or less or anything other than action in response to that Word, its
thinking and speaking would be empty, meaningless,
and futile. Because the Word of God is heard and
answered by theology, it is a modest and, at the same
time, a free science.* Theology is *modest* because its
entire logic can only be a human *ana-logy* to that Word;
analogical thought and speech do not claim to be, to
say, to contain, or to control the original word. But it
gives a reply to it by its attempt to co-respond with
it; it seeks expressions that resemble the ratio and
relations of the Word of God in a proportionate and, as
far as feasible, approximate and appropriate way. Theology's whole illumination can be only its human reflection, or mirroring (in the precise sense of "specula-
tion"!) ; and its whole production can be only a human
reproduction. In short, theology is not a creative act but
only a praise of the Creator and of his act of creation
—praise that to the greatest possible extent truly responds to the creative act of God. Likewise, theology is
free because it is not only summoned but also liberated
for such analogy, reflection, and reproduction. It is
authorized, empowered, and impelled to such praise of
its creator.

What is required of theological thought and speech,
therefore, is *more* than that they should simply conduct,
direct, and measure themselves by that Word. It goes
without saying that they must do that; and it is equally
true that such concepts are relevant to the relationship
of theology to the witnesses of the Word, of whom we

* It will be recalled that this was the substance of the first two
points of our introductory lecture, cf. pp. 6–9.

will speak next.* But for the relationship of theology to the Word itself, such concepts are too weak. The idea that autonomous man should be concerned with the response to the Word and its appropriate interpretation must be completely avoided. It cannot be simply supposed that man naturally stands in need of, and is subject to, the authority that encounters him in the Word. Before human thought and speech can respond to God's word, they have to be summoned into existence and given reality by the creative act of God's word. Without the *precedence* of the creative Word, there can be not only no proper theology but, in fact, no evangelical theology at all! Theology is not called in any way to interpret, explain, and elucidate God and his Word. Of course, where its relationship to the witnesses of the Word is concerned, it must be an interpreter. But in relation to God's Word itself, theology has nothing to interpret. At this point the theological response can only consist in confirming and announcing the Word as something spoken and heard prior to all interpretation. What is at stake is the fundamental theological act that contains and determines everything else. *"Omnis recta cognitio Dei ab oboedientia nascitur"* (Calvin).** Not only does this Word regulate theology and precede all theological interpretation; it also and above all constitutes and calls theology forth out of nothingness into being, out of death into life. This Word is the *Word of God*. The place of theology is direct confrontation with this Word, a situation in which theology finds itself placed, and must again and again place itself.

The Word of God is the Word that God *spoke, speaks,* and *will speak* in the midst of all men. Regardless of whether it is heard or not, it is, in itself, directed to all men. It is the Word of God's *work* upon men, for men,

* Cf. chapter 3, page 26.
** "True knowledge of God is born out of obedience."

and with men. His work is not mute; rather, it speaks
with a loud voice. Since only God can do what he does,
only he can say in his work what he says. And since his
work is not divided but *single* (for all the manifold
forms which it assumes along the way from its origin
to its goal), his Word is also (for all its exciting rich-
ness) simple and single. It is not ambiguous but unambiguous, not obscure but clear. In itself, therefore, it
is quite easily understandable to both the most wise and
the most foolish. God works, and since he works, he also
speaks. His Word goes forth. And if it be widely ignored
de facto, it can never and in no place be ignored *de jure.*
That man who refuses to listen and to obey the Word
acts not as a free man but as a slave, for there is no
freedom except through God's Word. We are speaking
of the God of the Gospel, his work and action, and of
the Gospel in which his work and action are at the same
time his speech. This is his Word, the Logos in which
the theological *logia,* logic, and language have their
creative basis and life.

The Word of God is Gospel, that is, the good word,
because it declares God's *good* work. In this Word, God's
work itself becomes speech.* Through his Word, God
discloses his work in his *covenant* with man, in the
history of its establishment, maintenance, accomplishment, and fulfillment. In this very way he discloses himself (both his holiness and his mercy) as man's father,
brother, and friend. At the same time, however, he
discloses his power and his eminence as the possessor,
Lord, and judge of man. He discloses himself as the
primary partner of the covenant—himself as *man*'s
God. But he also discloses *man* to be his creature, the
debtor who, confronting him, is unable to pay. Man is
lost in his judgment, yet also upheld and saved by his

---

* It is worth remembering in this context what was said about
this in point four of the last lecture, cf. pp. 10–12.

grace, freed for him and called by him to service and duty. He discloses man as God's man, as God's son and servant who is loved by him. Man is thus the other, the secondary, partner of the covenant. The revelation of the primacy of God and the station of man in the covenant is the work of God's word. This covenant (in which God is man's God and man is God's man) is the content of the Word of God; and God's covenant, history, and work with man are the contents of his Word which distinguish it from all other words. This Logos is the creator of theology. By it, theology is shown its place and assigned its task. Evangelical theology exists in the service of the Word of God's covenant of grace and peace.

What follows now is in no wise different from what has been said already, but it now says the same thing *concretely*. Theology responds to the Word which God *has spoken, still speaks,* and *will speak again* in the history of *Jesus Christ* which fulfills the history of Israel. To reverse the statement, theology responds to that Word spoken in the history of *Israel* which reaches its culmination in the history of Jesus Christ. As Israel proceeds toward Jesus Christ, and Jesus Christ proceeds out of Israel, so the Gospel of God goes forth. It is precisely the particularity of the Gospel which is its universality. This is the good Word of the covenant of grace and peace established, upheld, accomplished, and fulfilled by God. It is his Word of the friendly communion between himself and man. The Word of God, therefore, is not the appearance of an *idea* of such a covenant and communion. It is the Logos of this *history*, the Logos, or Word, of the God of Abraham, Isaac, and Jacob, who, as such, is the Father of Jesus Christ. *This* Word, the Word of this *history*, is what evangelical theology must always hear, understand, and speak of anew. We shall now try to delineate what this history declares.

First of all, this history speaks of a God who calls his own people to himself. Out of a tribal community which exemplifies all mankind, he calls his own people by acting upon it and speaking to it as *its* God and treating and addressing it as *his* people. The name of this God is *Yahweh:* "I am who I will be" or "I will be who I am" or "I will be who I will be." And the name of this people is Israel, which means—not a contender *for* God, but—"contender *against* God." The covenant is the encounter of this God with this people in their common history. The report of this history, although strangely contradictory, is not ambiguous. This history speaks of the unbroken encounter, conversation, and resultant communion between a holy and faithful God with an unholy and unfaithful people. It speaks of both the unfailing presence of the divine partner and the failure of the human partner that should be holy as he is holy, answering his faithfulness with faithfulness. While this history definitely speaks of the divine perfection of the covenant, it does not speak of its human perfection. The covenant has not yet been perfected. Israel's history, therefore, points beyond itself; it points to a fulfillment which, although pressing forward to become reality, has not yet become real.

At this point, the history of *Jesus,* the Messiah of Israel, commences. In it the activity and speech of the God of Israel toward his people, rather than ceasing, attain their consummation. The ancient covenant, established with Abraham, Isaac, and Jacob, proclaimed by Moses, and confirmed to David, becomes in Jesus Christ a new covenant. The holy and faithful God of Israel himself now calls into existence and action his holy and faithful human partner. In the midst of his people he lets one become man and espouses the cause of this man totally. With him he expresses the same solidarity that a father has with his son; he affirms that he, *God*, is identical with this *man*. Certainly, what is fulfilled in the existence and appearance, in the work and word of Jesus of Nazareth, is the history of God and his Israel, of Israel and its God. But the fulfillment of Israel's history is not its own continuation, as though God should raise up and call a new Moses, a further prophet, or a hero. Its fulfillment, instead, is the indwelling of God in this man, working and speaking through him. Anything less than this, obviously would be too little to fill up that vacuum. What the history of Jesus Christ confirms in the consummation of the history of Israel is *this event* in which the God of Israel consummates the covenant established with his people. The history of Jesus Christ is rooted deeply in the history of Israel, yet it soars high above Israel's history. It speaks of the realized unity of true God and true man, of the God who descends to community with man, gracious in his freedom, and of man who is exalted to community with him, thankful in his freedom. In this way "God was in Christ." In this way this one was and is the one who, although expected and promised, had not yet come forward in God's covenant with Israel. And in this way the Word of God was and is the consummation of what was only heralded in the history of Israel: the *Word* become *flesh*.

The history of Jesus Christ took place first and foremost for the benefit of Israel. It was the history of the covenant of God with Israel which attained its consummation in that subsequent history. And so God's Word, which was fully spoken in the history of Jesus Christ when it became flesh in him, remains first and foremost his concluding word to Israel. This ought never to be forgotten! Nevertheless, Israel was sent precisely as God's mediator to the nations; and this remains the meaning of the covenant made with it. The presence of God in Christ was the reconciliation of the world with himself in this Christ of Israel. In this consummating history, God's Word was now spoken in and with this, his work, which was done in and upon Israel. His Word remains a comforting announcement to *all* fellow men of the one Son of God, an announcement calling for repentance and faith. It is God's good Word about his good work in the midst, and for the good, of all creation. It is a Word directed to all peoples and nations of all times and places. The task of evangelical theology, therefore, is to hear, understand, and speak of the consummation of God's Word, both its intensive and its extensive perfection as the Word of the covenant of grace and peace. In the Christ of Israel this Word has become *particular*, that is, Jewish flesh. It is in the particularity of the flesh that it applies *universally* to all men. The Christ of Israel is the Saviour of the world.

This whole Word of God in Christ is the word to which theology must listen and reply. It is God's Word spoken both in the relation of the history of Israel to the history of Jesus Christ and in the relation of the history of Jesus Christ to the history of Israel. It is the Word of God's covenant with man—man who is alienated from God but who nevertheless is devoted to him, because God himself has interceded for man.

If theology wanted to do no more than hear and relate this Word as it appears in the *conflict* between God's faithfulness and man's unfaithfulness, theology would not respond to the whole Word of God. Should it limit itself to the conflict which would be characteristic for the history of Israel as such, theology would completely miss the central truth of this Word. The fact is, there is no history of Israel in itself and for its own sake. There is only the single history which, though it has its source in God's good will in overcoming Israel

—the "contender with God"—nevertheless hastens toward a goal. It hastens toward the history of Jesus Christ, the establishment of the human partner who, for his part, is faithful to the divine partner. In Israel's history there is no message that does not point beyond itself, that does not express its character as the Word of the divine partner at work in it. Every such message strives toward its consummation in the message of the history of Jesus Christ. Already containing this message within itself, Israel's history is to this extent already Gospel.

Theology would not respond to the whole Word of God if it wished only to hear and to speak of the Word become flesh. It would totally miss the truth of this Word if it proclaimed simply and solely the history of Jesus Christ, the Saviour of the world. As if the reconciliation of the world with God were made at the expense of, or in abstraction from, the promises given to Israel! If theology wishes to hear and repeat what God has said, it must remain attentive to what *happened* in Israel's history. What happened was the fulfillment and accomplishment of the *reconciliation* of Israel. The old, untiring, but now weary contender with God was reconciled by the will of the one true God. All the same, it was in this *Jewish* flesh that the Word of God now went forth into the whole world. "Salvation is from the Jews" (John 4:22). The covenant of God with man consists neither simply in the one nor simply in the other, but rather in the succession and unity of both forms of the history of the work of God. Similarly, the Word about this covenant goes forth in the same unity, since it is the Word of the selfsame God spoken both in the history of Israel and in the history of Jesus Christ. Their succession and unity form the whole Logos, and it is this unity of which evangelical theology must hear and speak. When theology fulfills this command, it takes and holds its post. To use a remarkable expression of Paul's, theology is then *logike latreia*. Not theology *only*, but among other services rendered in the church, theology *specifically* is committed to offer "reasonable service" to God.

A more precise determination of the place of evangelical theology requires that we take note of a definite (although not statistically definable) group of human beings. These enjoy a *special* and singular, indeed a unique, position in their relation to the Word of God. But their position is not special by virtue of a particular aptitude of sentiment or attitude toward the Word or by the fact that it might earn them particular favors, gratuities, or honors. Instead, it is special by virtue of the specific historical situation in which they are confronted by this Word, by the particular service to which the Word called and equipped them. They are the *witnesses* of the Word. To be more precise, they are its primary witnesses, because they are called directly by the Word to be its hearers, and they are appointed for its communication and verification to other men. These men are the *biblical witnesses of the Word*, the prophetic men of the Old Testament and the apostolic men of the New. They were contemporaries of the history in which God established his covenant with men. In fact, they became contemporary witnesses by virtue of what they saw and heard of this history. Other men, of course, were also contemporary witnesses of this history. But the prophets and apostles became and existed as eyewitnesses of those deeds done in their time, and *hearers of the Word* spoken in their time. They were destined, appointed, and elected for this cause by God, not by themselves; they were also commanded and empowered by him to speak of what they had seen and heard. They speak as men who in this qualified sense were *there*. The Logos of God in their witness is the concrete concern of evangelical theology. Though this theology has no direct information about the Logos, it nevertheless has, with the utmost certainty, this indirect information.

The prophetic men of the Old Testament witnessed Yahweh's action in the history of Israel, his action as father, king, lawgiver, and judge. They saw his free and constructive love, which nevertheless was a consuming love; in Israel's election and calling they beheld Yahweh's grace, and in his kind but also severe and wrathful direction and rule over this people they saw his untiring protest and opposition to the conduct of Israel, the incorrigible contender with God. Israel's history spoke to the prophets. In the manifold forms of this history they heard Yahweh's commands, judgments, and threats as well as his promises—not confirmations of their own religious, moral, or political preferences, or their optimistic or pessimistic views, opinions, and postulates! What they heard was, instead, the sovereign voice of the *God of the covenant:* "Thus says the Lord." This is the God who is constantly faithful to his unfaithful human partner. It was his own Word which these witnesses were enabled, permitted, and called to echo, either as prophets in the narrower sense of the term, or as prophetic narrators, or occasionally as lawyers, or as prophetic poets and teachers of wisdom. In giving their witness they, of course, listened to their predecessors as well, appropriating in one way or another their answers and incorporating them into their own. It was Yahweh's Word itself, as it was spoken in his history with Israel, which they brought to the hearing of their people. Naturally, each prophet also spoke within the limits and horizon of his time, its problems, culture, and language. They spoke, first of all, *viva voce,* but they also wrote down these words or had them written down so that they should be remembered by succeeding generations. The Old Testament canon is a collection of those writings which prevailed and were acknowledged in the synagogue. Their content was so persuasive that they were recognized as authentic, trustworthy, and authoritative testimonies to the Word of God. Evangelical theology hears witness of the Old Testament with the greatest earnestness and not merely as a sort of prelude to the New Testament. The classic rule is *Novum Testamentum in Vetere latet, Vetus in Novo patet:* the New Testament is concealed within the Old, and the Old Testament is revealed by the New. As long as theology preferred to neglect this rule, as long as it was content to exist in a vacuum by claiming exclusive orientation to the New Testament, it was continually threatened by a cancer in its very bones.

Nevertheless, theology must obviously focus its attention on the *goal* of the history of Israel, on the *prophetic* Word spoken in this history, on the *history of Jesus Christ* as it is witnessed to by the apostolic men of the *New Testament.* What these men saw and heard, what their hands touched, was the fulfillment of the covenant in the existence and appearance of the one human partner who was obedient to God. This fulfillment was the Lord who as a servant lived, suffered, and died in the place of the disobedient; the Lord who uncovered but also covered their folly, taking upon himself, and taking away, their guilt, uniting them and reconciling them with their divine partner. In the death of this Lord they saw the old contender *against* God overcome and vanquished, and in the life of this Lord, another man come forward, the new contender *for* God. In him they saw the hallowing of God's name, the coming of his kingdom, the fulfilling of his will on earth. In this event in time and space, in the "flesh," they were allowed to hear the Word of God in its glory, as a pledge, promise, warning, and consolation to all men. By Jesus' commission the apostles were sent out into the world in order to attest to all men that Jesus is this Word of God.

Once again, the subject and strength of their commission were neither their impressions of Jesus, their estimation of his person and his work, nor their faith in him. Instead, their theme was God's mighty Word spoken in Jesus' resurrection from the dead which imparted to his life and death power and control over all creatures of all times. The apostles spoke, told, wrote, and preached about Jesus as men who were in this way directly illumined and instructed. They spoke as men who had behind them the empty tomb and before them the living Jesus. Let it be noted that, *apart from* Jesus' history as the mighty Word in which God's reconciling act was revealed, the apostles lacked all interest in any other aspect of his history. They ignored any reality that might have preceded this history of salvation and revelation. There *was* simply no such reality; therefore they could not know or be concerned with any such hypothetical reality. Jesus' history was real, and real to *them*, pre-eminently as a history of salvation and revelation. For them, Jesus' reality was exclusively linked to their proclamation and based on his self-proclamation as *Kurios*, Son of God and son of man. It was neither a "historical Jesus" nor a "Christ of faith" which they knew and proclaimed, neither the abstract image of one in whom they did not yet believe nor the equally abstract image of one in whom they afterward believed. Instead, they proclaimed concretely the one Jesus Christ who had encountered them as the one who he was, even when they did not yet believe in him. Having their eyes opened by his resurrection, they were able to tell who he was who had made himself known to them *before* the resurrection. A twofold Jesus Christ, one who existed *before* and another who existed *after* Easter, can be deduced from New Testament texts only after he has been arbitrarily read into them. From the viewpoint even of "historical criticism," such an operation ought to be considered profoundly suspect. The origin, object, and content of the New Testament witnesses were and are the one history of salvation and revelation in which Jesus Christ is both God's deed and God's Word. Before and behind this history, all that the New Testament witnesses could reflect and contemplate was its commencement in the history of Israel as evidenced by the Old Testament. To *this* preceding history, and to this alone, they were constantly oriented. The New Testament *canon* is a collection of testimonies, fixed in writing and handed down, which relate the history of Jesus Christ in a way which proved itself authentic to the communities of the second, third, and fourth centuries. In contrast to all kinds of similar literature these communities approved the canon as the original and faithful document of what the witnesses of the resurrection saw, heard, and proclaimed. They were the first to acknowledge this collection as genuine and authoritative testimony to the one Word of God, at the same time taking over, with a remarkable naturalness and ease, the Old Testament canon from the synagogue.

We shall now attempt to clarify how evangelical theology is related to this biblical witness to the Word of God.

First of all, theology shares with the biblical prophecy and apostolate a common concern for human response to the divine Word. The witnesses of the Old and New Testaments were men like all others, men who had heard the Word and witnessed to it in a human way—in speech, vision, and thought that were human and conditioned by time and space. They were *theologians;* yet, in spite of having an identical orientation to an identical object, as theologians they differed widely from one another. Anything other than *their* intention, anything more or less than that, cannot be the substance of evangelical theology. In its study of the two Testaments, what theology has to learn as much as anything else is the method of a *human* thought and speech as they are oriented to the Word of God.

All the same, in the second place, theology is neither prophecy nor apostolate. Its relationship to God's Word cannot be compared to the position of the biblical witnesses because it can know the Word of God only at second hand, only in the mirror and echo of the biblical witness. The place of theology is *not* to be located on the same or a similar plane with those first witnesses. Since the human reply to the Word will in practice always consist partially in a basic question, theology cannot and dare not presume that its human response stands in some immediate relationship to the Word spoken by God himself. At that moment when everything depended on being present, scientific theology, as defined earlier in these lectures, is completely absent.

The position of theology, thirdly, can in no wise be exalted *above* that of the biblical witnesses. The post-Biblical theologian may, no doubt, possess a better astronomy, geography, zoology, psychology, physiology, and so on than these biblical witnesses possessed; but as for the Word of God, he is not justified in comporting himself in relationship to those witnesses as though he knew more about the Word than they. He is neither a president of a seminary, nor the Chairman of the Board of some Christian Institute of Advanced Theological Studies, who might claim some authority over the prophets and apostles. He cannot grant or refuse them a hearing as though they were colleagues on the faculty. Still less is he a high-school teacher authorized to look over their shoulder benevolently or crossly, to correct their notebooks, or to give them good, average, or bad marks. Even the smallest, strangest, simplest, or obscurest among the biblical witnesses has an incomparable advantage over even the most pious, scholarly, and sagacious latter-day theologian. From his special point of view and in his special fashion, the witness has thought, spoken, and written about the revelatory Word and act in direct confrontation with it. All subsequent theology, as well as the whole of the community that comes after the event, will never find itself in the same immediate confrontation.

Once and for all, theology has, fourthly, its position *beneath* that of the biblical scriptures. While it is aware of all their human and conditioned character, it still knows and considers that the writings with which it deals are *holy* writings. These writings are selected and separated; they deserve and demand respect and attention of an extraordinary order, since they have a direct relationship to God's work and word. If theology seeks to learn of prophecy and the apostolate, it can only and ever learn from the prophetic and apostolic witnesses. It must learn not this or that important truth but the one thing that is necessary—and with respect to this one thing on which all else depends, the biblical witnesses are better informed than are the theologians. For this reason theology must agree to let *them* look over its shoulder and correct its notebooks.

In the fifth place, the peg on which all theology hangs is acquaintance with the God of the Gospel. This acquaintance is never to be taken for granted; it is never immediately available; it can never be carried about by the theologian in some intellectual or spiritual pillbox or briefcase. The knowledge of Immanuel, the God of man and for man, includes acquaintance with the man of God. That he is Abraham's God, Israel's God, man's God— this is Yahweh's marvelous distinction from the gods of all other theologies. Theology has Immanuel—true God, true man—as its object when it comes from the Holy

Scriptures and returns to them. "It is they that bear witness to me." Theology becomes evangelical theology only when the God of the Gospel encounters it in the mirror and echo of the prophetic and apostolic word. It must also grasp God's work and word as the theme and problem of *its* thinking and speaking, in the same way that the Yahwist and Elohist, Isaiah and Jeremiah, Matthew, Paul, and John saw and heard this Word. Many other things, much that is interesting, beautiful, good, and true, could also be communicated and disclosed to theology by all sorts of old and new literature of other kinds. But with respect to the theme and problem that make it theological science, it will, for better or for worse, have to stick to this literature, the Holy Scriptures.

Nevertheless, in the sixth place, theology confronts in Holy Scriptures an extremely polyphonic, not a monotonous, testimony to the work and word of God. Everything that can be heard there is differentiated—not only the voices of the Old and New Testaments as such, but also the many voices that reverberate throughout both. It should be noted that the primary and real basis of this differentiation does not lie in the various psychological, sociological, and cultural conditions which existed for each witness. There is, of course, such a preliminary basis for differentiation in the profusion of biblical witnesses, in the various factors influencing their purposes and points of view, in the variety of their languages and the special theology of each. The primary basis, however, lies in the objective multiplicity and inner contrasts sustained within the motion of the history of the covenant which they recount and affirm. This motion is all-inclusive; it encompasses even its smallest elements, reflecting the interplay of unity and disunity between God and man as the witnesses disclose them. Therefore, although theology is certainly confronted with the one

God, he is One in the fullness of his existence, action, and revelation. In the school of the witnesses theology can in no way become monolithic, monomanic, monotonous, and infallibly boring. In no way can it bind or limit itself to one special subject or another. In this school theology will be oriented to the unceasing succession of different loci of the divine work and word, and in this way theological understanding, thought, and speech will receive their definite place. In the school of these witnesses theology inevitably begins to wander, though always with the same goal in mind. It migrates from the Old Testament to the New and returns again, from the Yahwist to the priestly codex, from the psalms of David to the proverbs of Solomon, from the Gospel of John to the synoptic gospels, from the Letter to the Galatians to the so-called "straw" epistle of James, and so on continually. Within all of these writings the pilgrimage leads from one level of tradition to another, taking into account every stage of tradition that may be present or surmised. In this respect the work of theology might be compared to the task of circling a high mountain which, although it is one and the same mountain, exists and manifests itself in very different shapes. The eternally rich God is the content of the knowledge of evangelical theology. His unique mystery is known only in the overflowing fullness of his counsels, ways, and judgments.

Theology responds to the Logos of God, in the seventh place, when it endeavors to hear and speak of him always anew on the basis of his self-disclosure in the Scriptures. Its searching of the Scriptures consists in asking the texts whether and to what extent they might witness to him; however, whether and to what extent they reflect and echo, in their complete humanity, the Word of God is completely unknown beforehand. This possibility must be seen and heard again and again, and this knowledge must be won from it and illuminated

repeatedly. The open, candid question *about this Word*
is what theology brings to the Bible. All other questions
are only conjoined and subordinated to this question;
they can present only technical aids to its solution.
Nowadays, of course, the "exegetical-theological" task is
often said to consist in the translation of biblical assertions out of the speech of a past time into the language
of modern man. The remarkable assumption behind this
project, however, seems to be that the content, meaning,
and point of biblical assertions are relatively easy to
ascertain and may afterward be presupposed as self-
evident. The main task would be then simply to render
these assertions understandable and relevant to the
modern world by means of some sort of linguistic key.
The message is all very well, it is said, but "how do you
tell it to the man on the street?" The truth of the matter,
however, is that the central affirmations of the Bible are
not self-evident; the Word of God itself, as witnessed to
in the Bible, is not immediately obvious in any of its
chapters or verses. On the contrary, the truth of the
Word must be *sought* precisely, in order to be understood
in its deep simplicity. Every possible means must be
used: philological and historical criticism and analysis,
careful consideration of the nearer and the more remote
textual relationships, and not least, the enlistment of
every device of the conjectural imagination that is
available.

The question *about the Word* and this question alone
fulfills and does justice to the intention of the biblical
authors and their writings. And in passing, might not
this question also do justice to modern man? If modern
man is earnestly interested in the Bible, he certainly
does not wish for its translation into his transitory
jargon. Instead, he himself would like to participate in
the effort to draw nearer to what stands *there*. This
effort is what theology owes to modern man and, above

all, to the Bible itself. "What stands there," in the pages of the Bible, is the witness to the *Word of God,* the Word of God in this testimony of the Bible. Just how far it stands there, however, is a fact that demands unceasing discovery, interpretation, and recognition. It demands untiring effort—effort, moreover, which is not unaccompanied by blood and tears. The biblical witnesses and the Holy Scriptures confront theology as the object of this effort.

When theology confronts the Word of God and its witnesses, its place is very concretely in the *community*,
not somewhere in empty space. The word "community,"
rather than "Church," is used advisedly, for from a theological point of view it is best to avoid the word
"Church" as much as possible, if not altogether. At
all events, this overshadowed and overburdened word
should be immediately and consistently interpreted by
the word "community." What may on occasion also be
called "Church" is, as Luther liked to say, "Christianity"
(understood as a nation rather than as a system of
beliefs). It is the commonwealth gathered, founded, and
ordered by the Word of God, the "communion of the
saints." These are the men who were encountered by the
Word and so moved by it that they could not withdraw
themselves from its message and call. Instead, they became able, willing, and ready to receive it as secondary
witnesses, offering themselves, their lives, thought, and
speech to the Word of God. The Word cries out for
belief, for this acceptance in recognition, trust, and
obedience. And since faith is not an end in itself, this
cry of the Word means that it demands to be proclaimed
to the world to which it is directed from the outset.

First of all, the Word insists upon being annunciated
by the choir of its primary witnesses. The community
represents the secondary witnesses, the society of men
called to believe in, and simultaneously to testify to, the
Word in the world. In this community, theology also has
its special place and function.

"I believed, and so I spoke." This attitude, taken over
from the psalmist by Paul, indicates the situation peculiar to the entire community as such, and in the last

analysis to each one of its members. The community is confronted and created by the Word of God. It is *communio sanctorum*, the communion of the saints, because it is *congregatio fidelium*, the gathering of the faithful. As such, it is the *coniuratio testium*, the confederation of the witnesses who may and must speak because they believe. The community does not speak with words alone. It speaks by the very fact of its existence in the world; by its characteristic attitude to world problems; and, moreover and especially, by its silent service to all the handicapped, weak, and needy in the world. It speaks, finally, by the simple fact that it prays for the world. It does all this because this is the purpose of its summons by the Word of God. It cannot avoid doing these things, since it believes. From the very beginning the community also expresses itself in spoken words and sentences by which, according to the summons of the Word, it attempts to make its faith audible. The work of the community consists also in its testimony through oral and written words, i.e., in the verbal self-expression by which it fulfills its commission of preaching, teaching, and pastoral counseling. And here begins the special service, the special function, of theology in the community.

In the area between the *faith* of the community and its *speech* a problem arises. What is the proper understanding of the Word that founds faith, the proper thought about this Word, the proper way to speak of it? Here "proper" does not mean pious, edifying, inspired, and inspiring; neither does it mean something that would satisfy the categories of everyday reason, thought, and speech. Although such properties would certainly be well suited to the speech of the community, they have no decisive significance for what this speech must achieve. What is at stake is the *quest for truth*. Take note that the quest for truth is not imposed on the community by the outside world (as the community in modern times permits itself, to a large extent, to be persuaded). The quest is not imposed in the name and authority of some general norm of truth or some criterion that is generally proclaimed as valid. Instead, it comes from within, or, more precisely, from above; it comes from the Word of God that founds the community and it faith.

The question about truth, therefore, is not stated in the familiar way: is it true that God exists? Does God really have a covenant with man? Is Israel really his chosen people? Did Jesus Christ actually die for our sins? Was he truly raised from the dead for our justification? And is he in fact our Lord? This is the way fools ask in their hearts—admittedly such fools as we are all in the habit of being. In theology the question about truth is stated on another level: does the community properly understand the Word in its purity as the truth? Does it understand with appropriate sincerity the Word that was spoken in and with all those events? Does the community reflect on the Word painstakingly and speak of it in clear concepts? And is the community in a position to render its secondary testimony responsibly and with a good conscience? These are the questions posed for the community, questions that are really urgent only for the people of God, and with regard to which no positive answer can ever or anywhere be taken for granted. Even the most able speech of the most living faith is a human work. And this means that the community can go astray in its proclamation of the Word of God, in its interpretation of the biblical testimony, and finally in its own faith. Instead of being helpful, it can be obstructive to God's cause in the world by an understanding that is partly or wholly wrong, by devious or warped thought, by silly or too subtle speech. Every day the community must pray that this may not happen, but it must also do its own share of earnest *work* toward this goal. This work is *theological* work.

There is no other way. In principle the community and the whole of Christianity are required and called to do such work. The question to be unceasingly posed for the community and for all its members is whether the community is a true witness. This question concerns, therefore, not only the community's speech but also its very existence. The community speaks in the surrounding world by the positions it assumes on the political, social, and cultural problems of the world. But the question of truth also concerns the community's order of worship, discipline, constitution, and administration, as well as its quiet ministerial work (which is perhaps not so quiet at all).

Since the Christian life is consciously or unconsciously also a witness, the question of truth concerns not only the community but the individual Christian. He too is responsible for the quest for truth in this witness. Therefore, every Christian as such is also called to be a theologian. How much more so those who are specially commissioned in the community, whose service is preeminently concerned with speech in the narrower sense of the term! It is always a suspicious phenomenon when leading churchmen (whether or not they are adorned with a bishop's silver cross), along with certain fiery evangelists, preachers, or well-meaning warriors for this or that practical Christian cause, are heard to affirm, cheerfully and no doubt also a bit disdainfully, that theology is after all not their business. "I am not a theologian; I am an administrator!" a high-ranking English churchman once said to me. And just as bad is the fact that not a few preachers, after they have exchanged their student years for the routine of practical service, seem to think that they are allowed to leave theology behind them as the butterfly does its caterpillar existence, as if it were an exertion over and done with for them. This will not do at all. Christian witness must always be forged anew in the fire of the question of truth. Otherwise it can in no case and at no time be a witness that is substantial and responsible, and consequently trustworthy and forceful. Theology is no undertaking that can be blithely surrendered to others by anyone engaged in the ministry of God's Word. It is no hobby of some especially interested and gifted individuals. A community that is awake and conscious of its commission and task in the world will of necessity be a theologically interested community. This holds true in still greater measure for those members of the community who are specially commissioned.

It is fitting that there should be a special theological activity, just as there are special emphases in other tasks of the community. The special theological science, research, or doctrine concentrates on the testing of the whole communal enterprise in the light of the question of truth. It functions to a certain extent vicariously and even professionally. Moreover, it is related to the community and its faith in roughly the same manner as jurisprudence is related to the state and its law. The inquiry and doctrine of theology, therefore, are not an end in themselves but, rather, functions of the community and especially of its *ministerium Verbi Divini*. Theology is committed directly to the community and especially to those members who are responsible for preaching, teaching, and counseling. The task theology has to fulfill is continually to stimulate and lead them to face squarely the question of the proper relation of their human speech to the Word of God, which is the origin, object, and content of this speech. Theology must give them practice in the right relation to the quest for truth, demonstrating and exemplifying to them the understanding, thought, and discourse proper to it. It must accustom them to the fact that here nothing can be taken for granted, that work, just as prayer, is indispensable. It also has the task of exhibiting the lines along which this work is to be conducted.

Theology would be an utter failure if it should place itself in some elegant eminence where it would be concerned only with God, the world, man, and some other items, perhaps those of historical interest, instead of being theology for the *community*. Like the pendulum which regulates the movements of a clock, so theology is responsible for the reasonable service of the community. It reminds all its members, especially those who have greater responsibilities, how serious is their situation and task. In this way it opens for them the way to freedom and joy in their service.

But in order to serve the community of today, theology itself must be rooted in the community of yesterday. Its testimony to the Word and the profession of its faith must originate, like the community itself, from the community of past times, from which that of today arose. Theology must originate also from the older and the more recent *tradition* which determines the present form of its witness. The foundation of its inquiry and instruction is given to theology beforehand, along with the task which it has to fulfill. Theology does not labor somewhere high above the foundation of tradition, as though Church history began today. Nevertheless, the special task of theology is a *critical* one, in spite of its relative character. The fire of the quest for truth has to ignite the proclamation of the community and the tradition determining this proclamation. Theology has to reconsider the confession of the community, testing and rethinking it in the light of its enduring foundation, object, and content.

The faith of the community is asked to seek understanding. Faith seeking understanding, *Fides quaerens intellectum,* is what theology must embody and represent. What distinguishes faith from blind assent is just its special character as "faith seeking understanding." Certainly, the assumption behind all this will be that the community itself may have been on the right track in the recent or remote past, or at any rate on a not altogether crooked path. Consequently, fundamental trust instead of mistrust will be the initial attitude of theology toward the tradition which determines the present-day Church. And any questions and proposals which theology has to direct to the tradition will definitely not be forced on the community like a decree; any such findings will be presented for consideration only as well-weighed suggestions. Nevertheless, no ecclesiastical authority should be allowed by theology to hinder it from honestly pursuing its critical task, and the same applies to any frightened voices from the midst of the rest of the congregation. The task of theology is to discuss freely the reservations as well as the proposals for improvement which occur to it in reflection on the inherited witness of the community. Theology says *credo,* I believe, along with the present-day community and its fathers. But it says *credo ut intelligam,* "I believe in order to understand." To achieve this understanding, it must be granted leeway for the good of the community itself. There are three points at which this freedom becomes important.

First of all, a tacit presupposition in our last lecture on the immediate witnesses of the Word of God was that we know *who* these witnesses are. We presupposed that both the community and theology know the identity of these witnesses who, since they are immediate, are authoritative for the community and its service. A further presupposition was that we know which scriptures must be read and interpreted as "holy" Scripture and acknowledged and respected as the theological norm. In fact, we do know this, for theology is a service in and for the community and springs from the tradition of the community. In this matter theology clings to that confession which is perhaps the most important and portentous of all Church confessions of faith, i.e., it clings to the selection of the various writings that confirmed themselves to the community as genuinely prophetic and apostolic witnesses. It was this selection that was unanimously accepted by the community of the late fourth century. The character of these writings as such witnesses is what the fathers of those days recognized and confessed by faith in God's Word, whose image and echo they perceived in them. To this knowledge and confession the community of every succeeding century has also committed itself, and with it, on the whole, it has had good and trustworthy experience. It is just this traditional canon which theology must first of all simply risk as a working hypothesis, for the decisive reason that it cannot refuse to join in that age-old act of faith if it is to be a service in and for the community.

The precise task of theology, however, is *credo ut intelligam*, "I believe in order to understand." In the fulfillment of this task, theology seeks to grasp and understand specifically one thing: the extent to which the canonical collection acknowledged by earlier generations actually *is* the canon of *Holy* Scripture. But how can this question be decided other than through knowledge of the content of those writings? How else can the rightness of traditional respect for the canon be tested other than by activating that working hypothesis? How else other than by questioning the texts of the Old and New Testaments as to whether and to what extent authentic witness of God's Word may be actually heard in them? How else, therefore, than in the careful investigation of those texts in the light of this question, by engagement in the exegetical circle that is unavoidable if those texts are to be understood? This investigation does not consist in premature anticipation but in expectation of an event, an event in which the authority of these texts announces itself. In this way theology sees, understands, and knows that the search for authentic witness to God's Word is fruitful only if pursued in the original canon. Theology knows also, however, that this search in the canon must be conducted with earnestness and total frankness. To be sure, theology always gropes to a great extent in the dark, with only a gradual, variable, partial knowledge. Nevertheless, even limited knowledge may convey, like a look through a keyhole, a glimpse of the riches of God's glory which is mirrored in the totality of the Biblical testimony.

In the second place, the thought and speech of the community have behind them a long history which is, in many ways, confused and confusing. The community's attention to the voice of the Old and New Testaments and to the Word of God witnessed by this voice was not always sensitive and accurate. It did not always withstand the temptation to listen to all sorts of strange voices as well, and often it listened almost entirely to them—to the voice of the old serpent. The dogmas, creeds, and confessions of the community are the documents of its resistance to this temptation and, at the same time, of its repenting return to its origins. They are the professions of its faith, formulated in opposition to all sorts of unbelief, superstition, and error. If theology did not take seriously the tradition of the community in the form of these documents of conflict, it would not be service in and for the community. In attempting to be equal to the quest for truth today, it must show both respect for the tradition and eagerness to learn from it. It must take note how one thing was occasionally defined and proclaimed as right and another anathematized as wrong *magno consensu,* by the consent of the majority of the fathers, during times of the beclouding of the Christian witness. Theology will often enough have occasion to wonder at the wisdom and determination of the decisions of the fathers that were made in their time and became significant for all times.

Nevertheless, the significance of tradition may not be simply taken for granted. *Credo,* indeed! But *credo, ut intelligam.* No dogma or article of the creed can be simply taken over untested by theology from ecclesiastical antiquity; each must be measured, from the very beginning, by the Holy Scripture and the Word of God. And under no circumstances may theology set out to appropriate creedal propositions merely because they are old and widespread and famous. If it is seriously committed to the quest for truth, it will forgo seeking the name and fame of an "orthodoxy" faithful to tradition. There is no heterodoxy worse than such orthodoxy! Theology knows and practices only *one* faithfulness. All the same, just this one faithfulness may perhaps prove to be also faithfulness to the confessions of the early Church and the Reformation for long stretches of the way, on the basis of the *intellectus fidei,* the understanding which is characteristic of faith.

Thirdly and finally, a brief comment is called for by the fact that the *history of theology* itself belongs to the tradition determining the community. As in all previous considerations, the *communio sanctorum* may and should be the starting point for understanding, even though this hypothesis is by no means easy to carry out (least of all in this case!). Nevertheless, the risk must be taken. The same hypothesis and risk apply particularly to the ruling theology of the past, whether of yesterday, of fifty, or of a hundred years ago. Time and again, the community grows used to living from what was said in it and to it yesterday; as a rule it lives from the Christian knowledge of yesterday. In the meantime, it is to be hoped, theology has advanced somewhat further, and what it supposes to know, what it ventures to think and to say *today*, will only seldom agree completely with what the fathers of yesterday thought and said. The far greater likelihood is that the newer theology will vigorously take exception to the fathers, especially to the immediate fathers. Even if this tension is justified by the vigorous nature of theological science, theology will still do well to keep in contact with its predecessors. For better or for worse, theology of yesterday is a bubbling source of the community and, above all, of theology itself. We will listen, therefore, with special attention precisely to those fathers of yesterday, interpreting them not only according to the critical rule, *credo ut intelligam,* but also in *optimum partem bona fide,* and making the best of them. By no means will we drop the problems which concerned them; instead, we will pursue them further, repeatedly meditating, considering, and reconsidering the very problems they posed, although at the same time no doubt putting them in the right perspective. Otherwise, theology might find the sons of today proving tomorrow to be enthusiastic rediscoverers and perhaps avengers of their grandfathers. The work of overcoming past weaknesses and errors, a work which was perhaps only apparently completed, would then have to begin all over again. May the good Lord preserve us from that!

We cannot overlook the fact that we ventured some very extraordinary statements in the last three lectures on the determination of the place of evangelical theology. Taken by themselves, of course, they may have been tolerably distinct and understandable, interrelated among themselves and also mutually confirming. Nevertheless, in their wholeness, as in their particulars, they were obviously statements that were not supported by what is usually considered sound evidence. They could not be derived from any points outside of the sphere of reality and truth which they themselves represented. They were not founded upon any results of a general science oriented to nature, man, the human spirit, or history, just as they had no dependence upon any philosophical foundations. Like the Melchizedek of the Letter to the Hebrews, each single sentence and all of them together were "without father or mother or genealogy." When we, nevertheless, ventured these statements, what power did we acknowledge? What is the power hidden within these assertions which establishes and illumines them? In other words, how does theology come to take and hold the place described by them—a place which seems to the onlooker to be situated in mid-air?

Let us recapitulate briefly in order to pinpoint this situation for ourselves. In our second lecture, "The Word," we ventured the statement that the history of Immanuel arose from the history of Israel and attained its goal in the history of Jesus Christ, and that this history, as such, was God's Word spoken to the people of all times and places. What a history! What a Word! What is the power that makes it so great a history and so bright a revelation? In our third lecture, "The Witnesses," we ventured the statement that there is a definite group of men, the biblical prophets and apostles, who directly heard the Word of that history. They were called by it to become its authentic and authoritative witnesses to the people of all times and places. How were these witnesses specially selected for such hearing? How were these men, no different from others, chosen for such proclamation? By what possible power? In our fourth lecture, "The Community," we ventured the affirmation that a whole group of men arose as secondary witnesses through the power of the Word spoken and entrusted to those earlier, primary witnesses. A community arose, the Church, destined and commissioned to proclaim the work and word of God in the world. What an extraordinary commission for a group of men! What is the power of their existence and action?

Obviously, all these assertions were ventured solely in order to describe the *place* of evangelical theology. Obviously, they had, as such, a strictly theological character and content. They could be only *theologically* guaranteed, only *theologically* intended and understood. What, then, is theology? According to these foregoing statements, by which we described its place, theology can be only theologically defined. Theology is science seeking the knowledge of the Word of God spoken in God's work—science learning in the school of Holy Scripture, which witnesses to the Word of God; science laboring in the quest for truth, which is inescapably required of the community that is called by the Word of God. In this way alone does theology fulfill its definition as the human logic of the divine Logos. In every other respect theology is really without support. While, seen from the viewpoint of an outsider, it hovers in mid-air, it depends actually upon God's living Word, on God's chosen eyewitnesses, and on the existence of God's people in the world. This dependence is its foundation, justification, and destination. The power of its existence is the power focused through those statements we have made about God's Word, God's witnesses, and God's people.

We will carefully refrain from speaking of a power *presupposed* either by us, in our theological assertions about the place of theology, or by theology itself in the form of any further theological statement. All would be betrayed, all would be false if we were to speak in this way. Theology cannot lift itself, as it were, by its own boot straps, to the level of God; it cannot presuppose anything at all concerning the foundation, authorization, and destination of its statements. It can presuppose no help or buttress from the outside and just as little from within. If theology wished to provide a presupposition for its statements, it would mean that it sought to make them, itself, and its work safe from any attack, risk, or jeopardy. It would presume that it could and must secure them (even if this presupposition was a tour de force, a *Deus ex machina* introduced in the form of a further theological statement). Precisely in this way theology would sell its birthright for a mess of pottage. Theology can only *do* its work. It cannot, however, seek to secure its operation. Its work can be well done only when all presuppositions are renounced which would secure it from without or within.

What can be arbitrarily presupposed, obviously stands at one's disposal. Were theology to *presuppose* the power sustaining its statements and itself (in the manner that mathematics presupposes the axioms supporting its theorems), then theology would assume *power* in its own right, superior to that first and fundamental power. Theology could then muster that power for its self-protection or at least place it on guard duty. The true power, which is powerful in its own right, defies being a potency which theology can possess and manipulate in its statements. Such presumed potency would be something like Münchausen trying to pull himself out of the bog by his own hair. In one way or another the very thing theology seeks (because in fact it needs it) would be lost whenever theology attempted to rely upon such an arbitrary presupposition.

We have to speak, therefore, of the real power that is *hidden* in theological assertions—hidden, unattainable, unavailable not only to the environment but also to the very theology which serves the community. This is the power *present* and *active* in what the affirmations of theology declare, in the history of salvation and revelation, in the hearing and speech of the biblical witnesses, in the being and act of the community summoned by them, and also in the work of theology when it testifies to these things. But this power is also totally superior to theology itself. It sustains and activates that whole event from the history of Immanuel down to the little tale in whose telling theology also, finally and at the last, has its existence and activity. In the telling of this tale, that hidden power prevents and forbids the slightest attempt to construct treacherous presuppositions. Most of all, it excludes the presumption that theology can vindicate itself. That power makes all arbitrary presupposing superfluous, since it is a *productive* power which replaces all safeguards stemming from other sources. It is power that produces security, of course—but just because its power is *creative* and *sufficient* to produce security, it is so effective that even the greatest theological master cannot, as it were, play with it as though it were one of his chessmen (perhaps the most powerful —the Queen). It is not endowed with a potentiality which the theologian knows and can exploit, as though he could overlook its origin, significance, and limits, The theologian does not have it in his control. This power is by no means a further theological assumption which he, much like a magician, could employ or not employ according to need or desire. He should be happy if, while brooding over his work, he hears the hidden power rushing, and finds his statements determined, ruled, and controlled by it. But he does not know "whence it comes or whither it goes." He can wish only to follow its work, not to precede it. While he lets his thought and speech be controlled by it, he gladly renounces the temptation to exert control over it. Such is the sovereignty of this power in the event of the history of Immanuel; such its sovereignty over and in the prophets and apostles; such its sovereignty in the gathering, upbuilding, and sending forth of the community; such its sovereignty as the hidden power of theological statements that describe and explain all this— statements such as we ventured in the three preceding lectures. No wonder that from the viewpoint of an outsider, these assertions seem to hover in mid-air, apparently crying for safeguards.

Is this true only from the viewpoint of an outsider? And do these assertions only *apparently* hover? It is precisely at this point that we must think further if we are to name this sovereign power by its true name. Is the phrase "hovering in mid-air" supposed to be something that characterizes theology only in its external aspect? Does it pertain to theology only apparently, as something probably harmful, from which theology should be acquitted as soon as possible? Still, "mid-air" could, above all, mean flowing, fresh, healthy air in contrast to all motionless and stagnant office air. And to "hover" in mid-air could also mean to be moved, borne, and driven by this flowing air. Who could actually wish that it were otherwise? It should be characteristic for theology to be borne and driven by this powerfully agitated and stirring air, not hindered by any safeguards existing ultimately and decisively in this very open air as its native habitat. All this should characterize theology if for no other reason than that such free mobility and movement are also the place of the community which lives from God's Word. On a higher level such motion is the place of the witnesses who directly hear and transmit the Word of God. And on a still higher level it is also the place where the history of Immanuel, as God's work, becomes God's Word. All this takes place in the realm of that freely moved and moving air, the gentle or stormy wind, the divine *spiratio* and *inspiratio*. According to the Bible, God's "spiration" and inspiration are the effective powers by which God discloses himself freely to men, making them accessible to himself and so on their part free for him.

The biblical name of this sovereign effective power is *ruach* or *pneuma*. And both terms mean, specifically, moved and moving air; they mean breath, wind, probably also storm, and in this sense, *spirit*. In the Latin *spiritus* and also in the French *esprit* this significance is rather clearly recognizable. In English the word should certainly not be reproduced by "Ghost" with its frightening proximity to "spooks." In German, unfortunately, *Geist* is a word which makes the dynamic significance of the biblical term altogether unrecognizable. Our use of the term, however, will be taken from the biblical axiom: "Where the Spirit of the Lord is, there is freedom" (II Cor. 3:17). The freedom of which we talk is God's freedom to disclose himself to men, to make men accessible to himself, and so to make them on their part free for him. The one who does that is the Lord God, who is the Spirit. There are also other spirits, those created good by God, such as the spirit natural to man. Moreover, there are demonic, erring, and disruptive spirits of annihilation which deserve nothing else than to be driven out. But none of these are that sovereign power of which we speak. Of none of them, not even of the best among them, can it be said that where they are, there is freedom. They must all be tested for the direction of their current, for their source from above or below. Above all, however, they must again and again be distinguished from the Spirit that, working in the *ambiance* of divine freedom, creates human freedom. In the Nicene Creed (as it was adopted by the Western Churches) the Spirit is called "the Holy One, the Lord and Giver of life," who "proceeds from the Father and from the Son, who together with the Father and the Son is adored and glorified." That is to say, the spirit is himself God, the same one God who is also the Father and the Son; he acts both as Creator and as Reconciler, as the Lord of the covenant. As this very Lord, however, he now dwells, has dwelt, and will dwell in men. He dwells not only *among* them but also *in* them by the enlightening power of his action. It is that flowing air and moving atmosphere in which men may live, think, and speak wholly and entirely freed from presuppositions—for they are men who know the spirit and are known by him, men called by him and obedient to him, his children begotten by his Word.

According to the second biblical saga of creation, God breathed into man "the breath of life," man's own spirit. This is the way the Spirit "spoke by the prophets," to use another phrase of the Nicene Creed. In this way John the Baptist saw the Spirit descend at the Jordan on the one who there, in solidarity with all sinners, accepted for himself the baptism of repentance. In this way the Spirit was the origin of the existence of the Son in the world of men—the Son who was *conceptus de Spiritu Sancto,* conceived of the Holy Spirit. In this way the spirit was the origin of the apostolate that proclaims the Son, as well as his nascent community. According to the Book of Acts, "suddenly a sound came from heaven like the rush of a mighty wind, and it filled all the house where they were sitting." By this power the disciples were enabled to speak of the mighty works of God and to be immediately understood even by those strangers who were present from every corner of the globe. It is in this manner that they spoke; and although they gave the impression of being drunk, it was as a result of this *spirare* and *inspirare* that the Word was understood and accepted by three thousand people. The Spirit *himself* was present, *God* the Spirit, the *Lord* who is the Spirit. This was his invasion, incitement, and witness to "what is in God" and "what has been given us by God," his power arousing and begetting the confession "Jesus is Lord!"

It was the Spirit whose existence and action make possible and real (and possible and real up to this very day) the existence of Christianity in the world. Up to this very day the Spirit calls into being the existence of every single Christian as a believing, loving, hoping witness to the Word of God. The Spirit does this certainly and irresistibly (for to wish to withstand him, when he steps in and acts, would be the one unforgivable sin), for he alone does this. "Any one who does not have the Spirit of Christ does not belong to him" (Rom. 8:9).

It is clear that evangelical theology itself can only be pneumatic, spiritual theology. Only in the realm of the power of the Spirit can theology be realized as a humble, free, critical, and happy science of the God of the Gospel. Only in the courageous confidence that the Spirit is the truth does theology simultaneously pose and answer the question about truth.

How does theology become the human logic of the divine Logos? The answer is that it does not *become* this at all; rather, theology may find that the Spirit draws near and comes over it, and that theology may then, without resisting, but also without assuming dominion over the Spirit, simply rejoice and obey its power. Unspiritual theology, whether it works its woe in the pulpit or from the rostrum, on the printed page or in "discussions" among old or young theologians, would be one of the most terrible of all terrible occurrences on this earthly vale. It would be so bad as to be without comparison with the works of even the worst political journalist or the most wretched novels or films. Theology becomes unspiritual when it lets itself be enticed or evicted from the freshly flowing air of the Spirit of the Lord, in which it alone can prosper. The Spirit departs when theology enters rooms whose stagnant air automatically prevents it from being and doing what it can, may, and must be and do.

The departure of the Spirit from theology can occur in two ways.

The first possibility is that theology, whether it is primitive or exceedingly cultivated, whether old-fashioned or, perhaps, most fashionable, will no doubt be practiced more or less zealously, cleverly, and probably also piously. In any case it will certainly be occasionally reminded of the problem of the Holy Spirit. Yet this theology does not muster the courage and confidence to submit itself fearlessly and unreservedly to the illumination, admonition, and consolation of the Spirit. It refuses to permit itself to be led by him into all truth. By such refusal, theology fails to give, in its inquiry, thought, and teaching, the honor due the Spirit of the Father and the Son that was certainly poured out over all flesh for its sake. One moment theology stands in out-and-out fear of the Spirit; in another it plays dumb, perhaps pretending to be better informed or else becoming obstinate in open opposition to him. As soon as the Spirit begins to stir within it, it suspects the danger of fanaticism; or it may rotate in circles of historicism, rationalism, moralism, romanticism, dogmaticism, or intellectualism, while "round about lies green and pleasant pasture."*

When theology poses and answers the question about truth in the above style and manner, it certainly cannot be serviceable to the community which, like itself, is totally dependent on the Holy Spirit. Its effect will be just the opposite! If theology is in the same situation as those disciples of John in Ephesus, who reportedly did not even know that there was a Holy Spirit, then theology must inevitably open the door to every possible, different, and strange spirit that aims at nothing other than to disturb and destroy the community, the church, and itself. Unpleasant consequences cannot and will not be lacking! Human criticism, mockery, and accusation, to be sure, cannot help theology when it is in this predicament. Only the Spirit himself can rescue theology! He, the Holy One, the Lord, the Giver of Life, waits and waits to be received anew by theology as by the community. He waits to receive from theology his due of adoration and glorification. He expects from theology that it submit itself to the repentance, renewal, and reformation he effects. He waits to vivify and illuminate its affirmations which, however right they may be, are dead without the Spirit.

The second possibility is that theology may know only too well about the rival power of the Spirit, which is indispensable to Christianity, to every Christian, and to it as well. Just because of this familiarity, theology may once again fail to acknowledge the vitality and sovereignty of this power which defies all domestication. In such a situation theology forgets that the wind of the Spirit blows where it wills. The presence and action of the Spirit are the grace of God who is always free, always superior, always giving himself undeservedly and

---

* From Goethe's *Faust*, Part One (scene in "The Study").

without reservation. But theology now supposes it can deal with the Spirit as though it had hired him or even attained possession of him. It imagines that he is a power of nature that can be discovered, harnessed, and put to use like water, fire, electricity, or atomic energy. As a foolish church presupposes his presence and action in its own existence, in its offices and sacraments, ordinations, consecrations and absolutions, so a foolish theology presupposes the Spirit as the premise of its own declarations. The Spirit is thought to be one whom it knows and over whom it disposes. But a presupposed spirit is certainly not the Holy Spirit, and a theology that presumes to have it under control can only be unspiritual theology.

The Holy Spirit is the vital power that bestows free *mercy* on theology and on theologians just as on the community and on every single Christian. Both of these remain utterly in need of him. Only the Holy Spirit himself can help a theology that is or has become unspiritual. Only the Spirit can assist theology to become enduringly conscious and aware of the misery of its arbitrary devices of controlling him. Only where the Spirit is sighed, cried, and prayed for does he become present and newly active.

Veni creator Spiritus! "Come, O come, thou Spirit of life!"* Even the best theology cannot be anything more or better than this petition made in the form of resolute work. Theology can ultimately only take the position of one of those children who have neither bread nor fish, but doubtless a father who has both and will give them these when they ask him. In its total poverty evangelical theology is rich, sustained, and upheld by its total lack of *presuppositions*. It is rich, sustained, and upheld, since it lays hold on God's promise, clinging without

* Title of a hymn by Heinrich Held, 1658.

skepticism, yet also without any presumption, to the promise according to which—not theology, but—"the Spirit searches all things, even the deep things of God."*

* At the conclusion of his delivery of the fifth lecture on "The Spirit," at Chicago and Princeton, Karl Barth added the following: "So much as an introduction to evangelical theology. But one thing remains to be added. Allow me to say it a little enigmatically and cryptically with the words of the Rebel General Stonewall Jackson, spoken at the hour of his death:

" 'Let us cross the river'—nobody knows whether he meant the Potomac or the Jordan—'and have a rest in the shade of the trees.' "

II THEOLOGICAL EXISTENCE

It is quite possible that in our previous lectures, in which we were concerned with the determination of the place of theology, theology itself might not yet have convincingly appeared as an element of real human life. In spite of all our warnings, it might still seem to be an abstract scheme or an hypostasis. It might even seem like one of the nameless virgins found on the façades of many medieval churches: whether clever or foolish, they are all the same made of stone. This impression must not go unchallenged.

Evangelical theology is always a history; it takes place in flesh and blood, in the existence and action of a human being, within the theologian in the narrower and broader sense of the term. It is precisely toward the *theologian* that we must now direct our attention. We must ask how theology encounters a man (to use the terminology popular nowadays) and how it confronts him, enters into him, and assumes concrete form in him. We are now approaching what may be called, with a slight and noncommittal bow before the gods of present-day philosophy, the "existentials" of evangelical theology. As in our preceding attempt to determine the place of theology, we will once again proceed in concentric circles. The first and most removed circle will now be designated by the word "wonder."

If anyone should *not* find himself astonished and filled with wonder when he becomes involved in one way or another with theology, he would be well advised to consider once more, from a certain remoteness and without prejudice, what is involved in this undertaking. The same holds true for anyone who should have accomplished the feat of *no longer* being astonished, instead of becoming continually *more* astonished all the time that he concerns himself with this subject. When he reconsiders the subject, however, such a man might find that astonishment wells up within him anew, or perhaps even for the first time. And this time such wonder might not desert him but might rather become increasingly powerful in him. That astonishment should remain or become wholly foreign to him is scarcely conceivable. But should that happen, both he and theology would fare better if he would devote his time to some other occupation.

A quite specific *astonishment* stands at the beginning of every theological perception, inquiry, and thought, in fact at the root of every theological word. This astonishment is indispensable if theology is to exist and be perpetually renewed as a modest, free, critical, and happy science. If such astonishment is lacking, the whole enterprise of even the best theologian would canker at the roots. On the other hand, as long as even a poor theologian is capable of astonishment, he is not lost to the fulfillment of his task. He remains serviceable as long as the possibility is left open that astonishment may seize him like an armed man.

In *general* terms, wonder occurs when someone encounters a spiritual or natural phenomenon that he has never met before. It is for the moment something uncommon, strange, and novel to him. He cannot even provisionally assign it a place in the previous circle of his ideas about the possible. For the time being he can only inquire into its origin and essence. Up to this point the concept of wonder is identical with the Socratic *thaumazein*—wonder that is astonished but receptive and desirous to learn. It has been justly said that this Socratic amazement is the root of all true science. The sense in which we have introduced the concept here likewise signifies an astonished and receptive desire to learn. Still, our concept involves more than a *provisional* hesitation and inquiry with respect to an uncommon, strange, and new phenomenon. Such phenomena might sooner or later, in the course of scientific progress, become something common, familiar and, to this extent, old and well known. They would then dispense man once again from his wonder, allowing him to divert his attention to other phenomena which, although at first astonishing, would certainly sooner or later cease to be so.

Another kind of wonder assumes control over a man when he takes up the subject of theology. Certainly this amazement also obliges a man to wonder and compels him to learn. But in theological wonder it is a sheer impossibility that he might one day finish his lessons, that the uncommon might become common, that the new might appear old and familiar, that the strange might ever become thoroughly domesticated. If a man could domesticate this wonder, he would not yet have taken the step into theology, or he would already have stepped out of it again. Man is never dismissed from the wonder that forms the sound root of theology. The object of theology never encounters a man routinely as does an ordinary object of the world. Instead, it constantly hovers on the edge of his circle of reflection, however large the circle may be. Progress in science, at this point, can only mean that theological hesitation and inquiry, in the face of the object of theology, more and more gain the upper hand. This captivation by the object will by no means ever lose its hold on man. If man becomes ever newly surprised then he becomes entirely and irrevocably a man who wonders.

"Wonderment" arises from "wonder." Whoever begins to concern himself with theology also begins to concern himself from first to last with wonders. Wonders are the occurrence, presence, and activity of what is basically and definitively incompatible and unassimilable to the norm of common experience. Theology is necessarily the logic of wonders, but it is not *only* the logic of wonders. It would cease to be theology if it should be ashamed of the fact that it is completely unable to categorize its object. It would not be theology should it refuse to confront the problem this inability poses.

A glance at the biblical stories about wonders or miracles will be instructive at this point. Such stories play a scandalously large role in the biblical testimony to the work and word of God. In the special sense of the biblical term, "wonders" are occurrences in time and space that have no analogies. Provisionally and non-technically defined, they are events that have no place in the generally familiar uninterrupted causal pattern of spatial and temporal events. Their "historical" verification (in the modern sense of this term) can apparently consist only in the observation and description of the certain fact that at an historically known place, occurrences of this kind have been reported. Anything more than this observation, whether positive or negative, would overstep the bounds of such historical verification. But narratives about just such occurrences are what form an integral part of the biblical witness to the history of the covenant of grace. This witness and its content would be violated if the biblical reports were reduced to the level of different kinds of occurrences.

The biblical stories, for instance, might be identified with occurrences which are understandable or "naturally explicable" within the causal relationships generally familiar and acknowledged as uninterrupted. Or they might be ignored as though they had not happened, simply because they are described as such incomparable occurrences. For the same reason, they might be reinterpreted as symbolic expressions of events that were really only immaterial, or as exuberant outbursts of the astonishing faith of the biblical witnesses.

Theology cannot employ either the first or the second or the third of the foregoing interpretations. It cannot allow itself to be sidetracked from the question about the work and word of God which are reflected in the biblical witness as it is *spoken*.

Those theologians and nontheologians hunt for the impossible and nonsensical who assume that the quest for the truth entrusted to theology must be identified with an inquiry into the possibility, verifiability, and explicability of the events that form the backbone of the Bible's message. Rather, theology has to recognize that the Bible's miracle stories have an essential place in the whole of the history narrated and explained by prophets and apostles. Theology must concern itself with the task of finding out what exactly is the place, the role, the relevance of those stories. There are theologians who prostrate themselves before the criteria of modern historiography; they are quick to label and to dismiss the miracle stories as sagas or legends. There are others who think and judge from within the framework and special character of the biblical witness; even when their attitude to the miracles is less skeptical, they are still in their own way also concerned with history. Both groups cannot possibly negate the essential and necessary function performed by the miracle stories in the whole and in decisive parts of the biblical message. What is the role of these stories?

As fundamentally *astonishing* stories, they function first of all in a formal way as a sort of *alarm signal*, which is the reason the New Testament likes to term them "signs." Scattered at times thickly and at other times more sparsely throughout the history of Immanuel, they alert the hearer and reader to a central fact: this history is concerned with a fundamentally *new* event which, although undoubtedly occurring within time and space, is not to be identified with other events occurring within the limits of time and space. This event springs up in their midst and is not some sort of continuation of what otherwise has happened or still happens in time and space. The Word which is spoken and speaks in this history is a fundamentally *new* word. Although it undoubtedly exists within time and space, it can be heard only in *this* history and is not to be compared with any other words. When the biblical miracle stories excite serious and relevant wonderment, they intend to do this as *signals* of something fundamentally new, not as a violation of the natural order which is generally known and acknowledged. This way they excite the type of wonderment from which no one can excuse himself once he has begun to pursue the subject of theology.

But what is the new element signaled by these miracle stories? Astonishment in itself might still be something like an uncomprehending, openmouthed marveling at the *portentum* or *stupendum* as such. To what do the following phrases point? " 'Rise, take up your bed and go home.' " " 'Come out of the man, you unclean spirit!' " " 'Peace, Be still!' " as was called out to a stormy sea. " '*You* give them to eat!' " as was said concerning the five thousand who were hungry in the wilderness. " 'Lazarus, come out!' " " 'He has risen, he is not here.' " According to the biblical testimony, what happened following such statements was always a change in the ordinary course of the world and nature which threatened and oppressed man. Though these changes were isolated and temporary, they were nevertheless radically *helpful* and saving. What took place were promises and intimations, anticipations of a redeemed nature, of a state of freedom, of a kind of life in which there will be no more sorrow, tears, and crying, and where death as the last enemy will be no more. What is communicated under the form of these little lights is always the reflected brightness of the great light which draws near to the men of the present in the form of hope. What is at stake is the summons, " 'Look up and raise your heads, because your redemption is drawing near' " (Luke 21:28). This kindling of the light of hope is what is really new; it is the really surprising element in the biblical miracle stories.

Nevertheless, these stories are only *one* element of the biblical witness to the history of Immanuel, even though, as such, they are admittedly indispensable and not to be overlooked. This history by no means exhausts itself in the fact that such stories occur within it. What is revealed in them is only the history's newness and the complete consolation it brings. This history is the indication of a new heaven and a new earth. These stories are only the *signs* of the new element that has its origin in this history, which continues to hurry forward toward its goal; they are not this new element itself. The new event, therefore, is not the water that was turned into wine at the marriage in Cana, or the young man who was restored to his weeping mother at Nain, or the food given to the five thousand in the wilderness, or the Sea of Galilee that so suddenly became calm, or the virginity of the mother of Jesus, or even his tomb that was found empty in the garden of Joseph of Arimathea. None of these is that new event which makes real and serious astonishment inevitable for anyone who takes up the study of theology. All those things could cause astonished frowns in the godless as well. The wonderment aroused by these signs, although it directs man's attention to another and better nature and world, would still not preclude the possibility of overlooking the really and decisively new event of which the biblical witness speaks. What is really and decisively new is the *new man*.

According to the biblical witness, Jesus acted by these miraculous deeds in the midst of other men as the Lord, servant, and guarantor for them all. In these deeds he proclaimed both himself and the righteousness and judgment of God. In them he revealed his glory. He himself is the new event, the great light of hope that has already come and will come again after having shined provisionally in these little lights. The new event is the world's reconciliation with God, which was announced in the Old Testament and fulfilled in the New Testament by Jesus Christ. The new event is the fulfilling and perfecting of the covenant between God and man. The new event is love, free grace, the unfathomable mercy with which God took up the cause of Israel, the criminal contender against God, and the cause of the whole rebellious and corrupted human race. He took up their cause by letting his Word become flesh, miserable and sinful flesh of sin like our own. The execution of his eternal counsel took place in a concrete act within time and space, not on the lofty pinnacle of some idea that might be easily comprehensible and persuasive for man. The Word became flesh in our place and for us, to overcome, take away, and eradicate the sin that separates us from God, the sin that is also the sting of death, the old element of our old nature and world. The new event is the name of God which is hallowed in this one person, in his obedience, service, life, and death. It is the kingdom come in him, established and active in him, God's will that in him is done on earth as in heaven. The new event is the pathway of children to their father, the way opened through him to all men and traversable for them all through the power of life of the Holy Spirit.

The new event, according to the biblical witness, is the history of *Jesus Christ* that concludes the history of *Israel.* Christ the Saviour is there! In a real and decisive sense, therefore, *he* is the miracle, the miracle of all miracles! Whoever takes up the subject of theology finds himself inevitably confronted with this miracle. Christ is that infinitely wondrous event which compels a person, so far as he experiences and comprehends this event, to be necessarily, profoundly, wholly, and irrevocably astonished.

The astonishment of the individual carries with it the fact that no one can become and remain a theologian unless he is compelled again and again to be astonished *at himself.* Last but not least, he must become for himself an enigma and a mystery. (*Nota bene:* the same applies even to those who are taking a minor in theology or who will always remain amateur theologians.) After all, who am I to be a theologian? It does not matter whether I am the best child of the best parents, perhaps having known, like Timothy (II Tim. 3:15), about the Holy Scriptures from the very time I began to think. It does not matter whether I have the cleverest mind or the most upright heart or the very best of intentions. Who am I to have put such trust in myself as to devote myself even remotely to the task of theology? Who am I to co-operate in this subject, at least potentially and perhaps quite actively, as a minor researcher, thinker, or teacher? Who am I to take up the quest for truth in the service and in the sense of the community, and to take pains to complete this quest? I have put such trust in myself as soon as I touch theology with even my little finger, not to speak of occupying myself with it more or less energetically or perhaps even professionally. And if I have done that, I have without fail become concerned with the new event and the miracle attested to by the Bible. This miracle involves far more than just the young man at Nain or the captain of Capernaum and their companions of whom the Gospels tell; far more than the Israelites' passage through the Red Sea, the wilderness, and the Jordan; far more than the sun that stood still upon Joshua's command at Gibeon. I have become involved in the *reality of God* that is only signaled by all these things. This is the God of Abraham, Isaac, and Jacob, who reveals himself in his Son through the Holy Spirit, who desired to be the God of man so that man might live as *his* man. I have become involved in the wonder of this God, together with all its consequences for the world and for each and every man. And whatever, however, and whoever I may be in other respects, I have finally and profoundly become a man made to wonder at himself by this wonder of God. It is another question whether I know what self-wonderment means for me, whether I am ready and able to subordinate my bit of research, thought, and speech to the logic of this wonder (and not in reverse order!). But there can be no question about one fact: I find myself confronted by the wondrous reality of the living *God*. This confrontation occurs in even the most timid and untalented attempt to take seriously the subject in which I have become involved or to work theologically at all, whether in the field of exegesis, Church history, dogmatics, or ethics.

In one way or another I am obliged to consider the question of the wonder of God. I may perhaps attempt to steal away from the confrontation and preoccupation with this wonder. But I can no longer be released from this confrontation. Theology undoubtedly gives the man who is concerned with it something like a *character indelebilis,* an indelible quality. Whoever has eyes to see will recognize even at a distance the man who has been afflicted and irreparably wounded by theology and the Word of God. He will be recognizable by a certain earnestness and humor, whether genuine or spurious, real or only pretended. But the process and the way in which

it was possible for him to become such a man will always
be hidden, even from the theologian himself. This process
will remain a deeply wondrous enigma and mystery. I no
doubt know and recognize myself quite passably in all
my other opinions and inclinations, in all my other real
or fancied or desired possibilities. By birth and nature
we are indeed all rationalists, empiricists, or romanticists
in some sort of mixture, and we have no occasion to be
astonished at ourselves in this respect. All that is simply
a fact. But I become, am, and remain something unknown, a different person, a stranger, when I am counted
worthy to be permitted and required to wonder with
respect to the wonder of God. And this is what happens
when I become concerned with theology. How could my
existence with this permission and demand to wonder
ever become an everyday, familiar, and trite fact? How
could this attribute of my existence ever become transparent to me?

To become and be a theologian is not a natural process
but an incomparably concrete fact of grace. This is so,
precisely from the viewpoint of the radical and fundamental astonishment in which alone a man can become
and be a theologian. While looking only at himself, a
man can *not* recognize himself as a recipient of grace,
and consequently he cannot take pleasure and pride in
himself. As the recipient of grace, a man can only become active in gratitude. If anyone supposed he could
understand himself as such a receiver of grace, he would
do better to bid theology farewell and devote himself to
some other sort of activity. There he might shut his
eyes to the wonder of God (if he can) and would also
not need to wonder at himself (if he is able). But perhaps he will find no other activity in which he might
effectively and definitively elude theology, the wonder of
God, and, consequently, his astonishment at this wonder
and at himself.

Wonderment? If this concept is to be an adequate description of what makes the theologian a theologian, it immediately requires concrete delimitation and deepening. Even in the expanded interpretation we have given it, "wonder" could still be misunderstood as mere "admiration."

Admiration is something with considerable and perhaps promising theological significance. Johann Gottfried Herder once read and interpreted the Bible with admiration as a document of ancient Oriental poetry, and after long decades of a thoroughly arid enlightenment, such a view of the Bible was for many a stimulating and exciting possibility. The young Schleiermacher, in his turn, summoned the cultured despisers of religion to admiration of the phenomenon of religion in general. A century later, what intensely interested us youths of that day in the works of Duhm or Gunkel was their admiration for at least the prophets and psalms, at any rate, as the high point of the world of the Old Testament. Paul Wernle was regarded by his students as an unforgettable teacher because of his admiration (following in the footsteps of Thomas Carlyle) for the human person of Jesus as well as (with a few reservations) for the apostle Paul, the Reformers, and a throng of figures from Church history who appealed to him. And Rudolf Otto also was able to describe to us quite impressively the "Holy" as a *fascinosum*. No doubt more was involved in all this than "admiration" alone. There was a certain justification for the fact that the concept of "experience," brought to vogue by Wilhelm Herrmann and others, was in all our mouths about 1910 and already pointed beyond mere admiration. But at all events, theology cannot and may not in any case remain content with *mere* admiration if it is to be a serious affair.

What we termed in the previous lecture the inevitable wonderment of theology dare not be understood as but a species of intellectual sensibility. This would hold true even if its theme—transcending the aforementioned line of modern Protestant theology—were not merely the wonder of religious personalities or religious life and conduct but the wonder of God himself. Of course, as Anselm of Canterbury knew, since there is a beauty of God there is also a *pulchritudo* of theology which cannot be ignored. But theological observation of God cannot be a genial and detached survey. Theology cannot be an easygoing (or even interested and perhaps fascinated) contemplation of an object. For in the last analysis the attitude of the more or less enraptured subject toward this object might remain indifferent or skeptical, if not spiteful. If this object allowed its beholder to protect himself behind a fence of reservations, it would not at all be the wonder of God of which we spoke. When this object arouses wonderment of the type we have described, transforming the man whom it involves into an astonished subject, this man also becomes *concerned*. This is the further determination of theological existence which must now especially occupy our attention.

When a man becomes involved in theological science, its object does not allow him to set himself apart from it or to claim independence and autarchic self-sufficiency. He has become involved in theology, even if his reasons for such involvement may have been very superficial, or, indeed, utterly childish. Certainly, he never knew beforehand what a risk he was taking, and he will certainly never fully grasp this risk. But at any rate he has taken this step. He is a theologian because he finds himself confronted by this object. His heart is much too stubborn and fearful, and his little head much too weak, but he cannot merely dally or skirmish with this object. The consequences can no longer be avoided. This object disturbs him—and not merely from afar, the way a lightning flash on the horizon might disturb one. This object seeks him out and finds him precisely where he stands, and it is just *there* that this object has already sought and found him. *It met, encountered, and challenged him.* It invaded, surprised, and captured him. It assumed control over him. As to himself, the light "dawned" on him, and he was ushered up from the audience to the stage. What he is supposed to do with this object has become wholly subordinate to the other question about how he must act now that this object obviously intended to have, and already has had, something to do with him. Before he knows anything at all, he finds *himself* known and consequently aroused and summoned to knowledge. He is summoned to *re-search* because he finds himself searched, to thinking and reflection because he becomes aware that someone thinks of him, to speech because he hears someone speak to him long before he can even stammer, much less utter a coherent sentence. In short, he finds himself freed to be concerned with this object long before he can even reflect on the fact that there is such a freedom, and before he has made even an initial, hesitant, and unskilled use of it. He did not take part in this liberation, but what happened was that he was *made* a direct participant in this freedom. When he dipped even the tip of his toe into the waters of this Rubicon or Jordan (or whatever the river may be called), he was already both compelled and allowed to pass through to the other side. Perhaps frowning, confused and shocked, and definitely altogether incompetent, he is all the same on the other shore from which there is no return. The fact is now: *Tua res agitur,* the matter concerns you!

What am I describing? The genesis and existence of a prophet? No, but simply the entirely peculiar character of the theologian's origin and life. The genesis and existence of some great theologian? Nonsense—because what can "great" mean? There may be great lawyers, doctors, natural scientists, historians, and philosophers. But there are none other than *little* theologians, a fact that, incidentally, is fundamental to the "existentials" of theology. Even he who is little in the field of theology is overwhelmed by this object. No one is concerned with this science, even at the most remote sphere of his activity or even as a clumsy dilettante, over whom this object does not irresistibly gain the upper hand. While not possessing it at all, no man is confronted by this object who is not possessed by it. The theologian for his part becomes, whether willingly or unwillingly, consciously or unwittingly, quite definitely not only a fascinated but also a concerned man.

Tua res agitur! You are concerned! What does "you" mean? We shall attempt to give three answers that once again are related to one another like three concentric circles. All represent basically a single answer, yet each of them has its own weight in its own place and manner.

1. Theological existence, like the existence of every human being, is existence in the present epoch of the cosmos. It occupies a specific fraction of the secular time that has not yet come to its end. It is like a ring in the chain of the ever continuing generations of the human race, a ring that today is strained and tested for its durability. It lives and perseveres in its own situation as an active and passive subject of the history of man and society. The little theologian likewise exists, in common with all other men, as a creature allotted his particular possibilities by his cosmic situation and determination. In his environment he is harassed by his own special needs, but in one way or another he has also a

share in special tasks and hopes. Though his special situation affords him no advantage, he has also no disadvantage in comparison with all the others; he is neither mightier nor weaker than they. But he is confronted with the Word of God expressed and audible in God's work, and it is this which he cannot suppress.

Wittingly or unwittingly, as a theologian he has exposed himself to this Word. *He,* at any rate, cannot possibly hide from himself the fact that this Word is directed precisely to his own world. This Word concerns mankind in all times and places, the theologian in his own time and place, and the world in its occupation with the routine problems of the everyday. This Word challenges the world in which X, Y, and Z appear—with their own big words—to have the say and to determine the lot of all men and things as well as the lot of theologians. While the theologian reads the newspaper, he cannot forget that he has just read Isaiah 40 or John 1 or Romans 8. *He,* at any rate, cannot suppress the knowledge that the Word of God speaks not only of an infinitely deeper need but also of an infinitely higher promise than the sum total of all the needs and promises characteristic of his time and place. He cannot suppress his awareness that this Word is not only the word of God's verdict and judgment upon all human existence and its perversion, but much more the word of God's gracious covenant with man. He knows that this covenant is not only planned but already established and fulfilled. The Word to which he is exposed treats of man's completed reconciliation with God. It speaks of the righteousness by which all human unrighteousness is already overcome, of the peace that has made all human wars (whether cold or hot) already superfluous and impossible, of the order by which a limit has already been set to all human disorder.

And last of all, the man encountered by the Word

cannot ignore the fact that, along with all time, his present time moves toward a goal where all that is now hidden will be revealed. He knows that this time was and is the time of Jesus Christ and therefore—in spite of every apparent contradiction—a time of grace. The fact cannot escape him that what is involved in the Word is not the proclamation of some sort of principle, a new moral and political program, or a better ideology. But what is involved and meant by that Word is rather and immediately the woe and the salvation which are eternal and thus also temporal, heavenly and for this reason also earthly, coming and therefore already present. By that Word are expressed and declared: woe and salvation to the Europeans *and* the Asians, the Americans *and* the Africans, woe and salvation to the poor rigid Communists *and* woe and salvation to the still poorer (because still more rigid) anti-Communists, woe and salvation to us Swiss as well, to our self-righteousness which is exceeded only by our business acumen, our profound anxiety, our milk and watches, our tourist trade, our narrow-minded rejection of voting rights for women, and our somewhat childish desire for a few choice atomic weapons.

The content of God's Word is his free, undeserved Yes to the whole human race, in spite of all human unreasonableness and corruption. And the theologian cannot by-pass this Word, even if everyone else among his all too self-satisfied and all too troubled fellow creatures tried perhaps to by-pass it. In this attempt to dodge the Word, they will not succeed. A theologian is he who has once and for all been compelled and permitted to face and accept, in an especially concrete manner (possibly even professionally), the challenge of the Word of God. This Word cannot possibly do otherwise than examine, involve, and concern him, piercing him to the heart (Acts 2:37)—even him who exists as a present-day man in the present world, his share of the burdens of the present generation. How else should he actually exist in the world (whatever the practical consequences may be) than as one who is involved, concerned, and really pierced through the heart by this Word?

2. All the same, theological existence does not swim alone in this world's seas, drifting with the waves or battling against them. It is not only shared with other human beings; it is also *Christian* existence inasmuch as it is existence in the *community*, called together and sustained by the witness of the Old and New Testaments to the Word of God.

No one can be a theologian without at some point participating totally in the problematic aspects of Christianity. The theologian participates in the life of Christianity, which is always threatened by destruction, although again and again rescued from it. He participates in its partially necessary and partially accidental, but mainly self-incurred, isolation from those sections of humanity which do not belong to it, and from the spiritual, psychical, and physical powers that rule mankind. He participates also in its fortunate or less fortunate attempts to break out of this isolation. He shares the limited respect theology sometimes receives, as well as the sad disrespect and often worse adulation that are accorded it. He participates in its schisms and in its longing for unity, in its obedience as well as in its indifference, and finally in its lassitude, which often masquerades as busyness. He is a Christian while he is a member, perhaps, of a state church, or of a free church, or as a Lutheran or Reformed or Methodist or Roman Catholic. Perhaps he takes pleasure in the old-time religion, or in religious progress, or in the social or aesthetic assimilation achieved by the special brand of his own Christianity. Christianity admittedly exists in such sheer particularities. To a large extent, this may appear at first glance to be justifiable; but the fact is notorious that, in many respects, it cannot be justified.

This is the way each theologian exists in his place. However, wherever he may be situated and whatever stand he may take, in the last analysis, he can *not* really exist in such particularity or feel himself ultimately at home with them. Regardless of where and how he may stand, the quest for truth has been assigned to him as a member of the people chosen by the truth itself and called through its revelation. Whether he knew what he was doing or not, he has taken up the task of reflecting on the question about truth. This was the question posed for that people from the very beginning and in all its subsequent historical forms. Regardless of how this people may fare or what position it may take, it stands and falls by the answer to this question. Compared with the question about truth, all the special problems of this people can be only child's play. Nevertheless, when seen in the piercing light of that question, even the minutest problem about the community's service, order, or proclamation can receive ultimate and greatest weight. Everything that happens or does not happen in the life of this people directly concerns the theologian; whether it happens in one way or another, well or ill, it becomes inexorably his concern. And this occurs in such a way that he may neither overestimate nor underestimate anything, neither take anything too lightly nor count anything too tragic. He cannot cease to think along with this community and, in certain circumstances, also to speak, in both respects quite sharply but also quite cheerfully on major or minor points. He does this not because he is personally such an important or even sovereign and versatile man. He does this simply because the one Word of the one sovereign Lord of all Christianity has so pursued him that he cannot evade the vision of the one thing by which alone the people of

God can and may live. The one Lord over all the forms and predicáments of Christianity has so frontally attacked him—the "little" theologian—regarding his function within the community, that he cannot shake off this one thing—not even in his sleep, much less in the supposed or real strengths and weaknesses, heights, and depths of his life. The judgment pronounced upon the community by this Word falls upon him as well; however, he is also uplifted by the promise which is given the community and sealed by the fact that it may live from this Word.

3. Theological existence is exclusively the *personal* existence of the "little" theologian. He exists not only in the world and not only in the community but also simply by himself. And since the Word of God, which is the object of theology, is concerned with the world and the community in the world, it is concerned also with the theologian in his existence for himself. What is involved is the judgment which falls upon him and the grace which is granted him, his imprisonment and liberation, his death and his life. What is involved is, finally and conclusively, he himself in everything which he as a theologian must know, investigate, and consider concerning the quest for truth. It would not, however, be fitting to suppose that what is involved is first and foremost he himself, and then only subsequently and at a certain remove the community, and finally, at a still greater distance, the world. Such a sequence might suggest that subjectivity was the truth (according to the statement of Kierkegaard, which is at the very least open to misunderstanding). If the community and the world were not involved, he himself could not be involved. For only in the community and the world is he the one who he is; and just because the community and the world are involved, he, too, is finally and conclusively involved.

What is implied by the relationship between God's covenant of grace and the human race is the theologian's election, justification, sanctification, and calling. His prayer and work are included, his joy and sorrow, himself in his relation to his neighbor, the unique opportunity of his short life, his stewardship with the capabilities and possibilities given to him, his relation to money and possessions, to the opposite sex (in marriage and in every encounter), to his parents and children, to the morality and immorality of his environment. In the last analysis, he is the one who is concerned, questioned, and accused by God's Word; judged and justified, comforted and admonished, not only in his function and role among his fellow men, but also personally in his existence for himself. He himself is the one whom God makes an "I" by addressing him as a "Thou."

The story is told that the once famous Professor Tholuck of Halle used to visit the rooms of his students and press them with the question, "Brother, how are things in your heart?" How do things stand with you yourself?—not with your ears, not with your head, not with your forensic ability, not with your industriousness (although all that is also appropriate to being a theologian). In biblical terms the question is precisely, "How are things with your *heart?*" It is a question very properly addressed to every young and old theologian!

The question might also read: "Adam, where are you?" Are you perhaps—in your interior and exterior private life—fleeing from the One with whom you as a theologian are pre-eminently concerned? Have you hidden yourself from him in the shrubbery of your more or less profound or high-flown contemplation, explication, meditation, and application? Are you perhaps living in a private world which is like a snail's shell, considering yourself deeply and invisibly hidden beneath and behind all externals, while on closer view your life might prove

to be that of an unenlightened, unconverted, and un-
controllably corrupted and savage little bourgeois or
gypsy? But this "perhaps" is impossible! Let no one
think that on such a basis he would be capable of any
properly free and fruitful theological inquiry, thought,
and speech! There is no avoiding the fact that the living
object of theology concerns *the whole man*. It concerns
even what is most private in the private life of the theologian. Even in this sphere the theologian cannot and
will not flee this object. If this situation should not suit
him, he might, of course, prefer to choose another and
less dangerous discipline than theology. But he should
be aware that it is characteristic for the object of theology to seek out every man in every place sooner or
later (see Psalm 139). It will seek him out wherever he
may be and pose to him the same question. Therefore, it
would probably be simpler to remain a theologian and
learn to live with God's claim upon even the most intimate realms of the theologian's humanity.

In our sixth lecture we isolated "wonderment" as the
first element that makes the theologian a theologian. We
meant wonderment before the unprecedented newness of
the object of theology. We described "concern" as a
second element in our seventh lecture. Concern is
inevitable because of the unique actuality, indeed aggres-
siveness, of the object with which man becomes involved
in theology. But this object also demands that involvement cannot stop simply at the point of even the greatest
concern (or of "the deepest experience," as would have
been said fifty years ago). When this object concerns
man in its peculiarly penetrating and intimate way, it
desires something special not only *for* him but also *from*
him. It encourages him, it sets him on his feet, and it
frees him, but it also claims him and tells him to walk
and make use of the freedom that has been granted him.
The event of "commitment" is the third element that
makes the theologian a theologian.

It is splendid and beautiful to be assigned a duty by
the God of the Gospel who is the object of evangelical
theology, but it is also demanding, exalting, and finally
terrifying. A *nobile officium,* a noble charge, is confided
and entrusted to man; but this charge implies that he is
expected to fulfill his ministry. He is privileged to do
what is expected of him. But he also *must* do what he is
chosen to do.

Since the concern which claims the theologian even in
his private life is total, his commitment is also total.
Commitment begins with the theologian's wonder and
is directly related to his concern. It comprehends, indeed, his whole existence.

The theologian's existence clearly involves a responsibility imposed by his special function. His existence is endowed with a special freedom and called to a special exercise of this freedom. What interests us is the degree to which the theologian is rendered responsible within his science by its object. He is freed and claimed for a specific kind of perception, inquiry, thought, and speech. He has not devised and chosen this mode of perception himself; rather, it was forced upon him when he took up the task of theology. If he desires to be and remain faithful to that task, he must appropriate its way of thought, practicing it steadfastly and remembering or letting himself be reminded of it continually. What is involved is the method peculiar to theology. The word "method," though burdensome, is unavoidable in the sense of defining a procedural regimen which corresponds to the task of theology. Expressed in other terms, what is involved is the *law* according to which the theologian must proceed. By such a law the theologian is bound, beyond all mere wonderment and concern, to knowledge and confession of his proper object.

Neither the word "method" nor the word "law" is to be understood as a burden laid upon the theologian, a prison regulation hindering him or, in short, a compulsion placed upon him. What is involved is the method or law of freedom by which he must inquire, think, and speak. His commitment can only be a compulsion for him if he has not yet dedicated himself consciously and determinedly to, or for some reason or other has deserted, the object of his science. When dedicated to the Word and work of God, he exists as a free man precisely because of the respect he pays to the method and law of his science. The only burden, compulsion, and Babylonian captivity would be for him the necessity of pursuing another method, or respecting and fulfilling an alien law of knowledge—however, just such an alien law is what he has left behind when he sets out on the path of the *intellectus fidei.*

We must now briefly draw some conclusions about the regulation of the *intellectus,* about the type of knowledge to which the theologian is bound, freed, and summoned. We will reserve for the next lecture the problem posed by the fact that this is the *intellectus fidei,* the understanding of *faith,* and not simply the *intellectus* independent of *fides.* At this juncture, however, we will only inquire into the character of the *intellectus.* Here, three points must be set forth and confirmed.

1. The work and word of God which form the object of theology are a *unity.* It should not be forgotten, of course, what was said in our second and third lectures, that his is no monolithic work and no monotonous word. Rather, this unity is the work of the living God—a *unity* of rich and diverse forms, all of which are evident in the witness of Scriptures. Heights and depths, things great and small, near and remote, special and universal, internal and external, visible and invisible, are all enclosed within the reality and revelation of God's covenant with man. One beholds in Scriptures God's eternal being within himself and his being in time for us, his election and rejection, his mercy and judgment, his action as creator, reconciler, and redeemer, in effect, his heavenly and his earthly politics; and one also beholds God's creature—good, fallen, and renewed after God's image, replete with the nature appointed him and the grace granted him, his transgression and obedience, his deserved death and promised life. And in all this there is also past, present, and future.

All these exist together: the one not without the many and the center not without its infinite circumference, although no one point of the circumference is identical or interchangeable with any other. None is insignificant, unimportant, or dispensable; none is without its special

truth and worth. There is none that does not represent
and reflect the whole; and there is none concerning
which, proper or improper knowledge might not have
crucial consequences. But there is also none that is able
to step outside of the unity of the work and word of
God which surround and determine it. None may be
observed, understood, and interpreted in isolation for
its own sake, being treated as a secondary focus, perhaps even being made the center itself. The object of
theological science in all its disciplines is the work and
word of God in their fullness, but in their fullness they
are also the *one* work and word of God. This work and
word are Jesus Christ, the *one* who was crowned as king
of the Jews and Saviour of the world, who represents the
one God among men and man before the one God. He is
the *one* servant and Lord who was expected, who arrived, and is now truly expected. Oriented to him who
is its starting point and its goal, theological knowledge
becomes a knowledge that articulates the unity of the
manifold.

The *intellectus fidei* is engaged in gathering, although
it abstains from equalizing, stereotyping, or identifying.
While it gives every point of the circumference its special due, it brings together all parts from their own
individual centers to their common center. Theology
finds itself committed, freed, and summoned to such
knowledge. In the theological act of knowledge, seeing
is doubtless an attentive and exact gaze toward one or
another special form of the object; as such, it is also
sight that views one form together with the others.
What is decisive is that it is an insight into the one
object which presents itself now in this, now in that,
form, or an insight into one peculiar form which has
become a form of the one object. In the act of theological
knowledge, every view, insight, and vision is attentively
and accurately concentrated upon this or that form.

But also a *syn-opsis,* a seeing together of different forms, takes place. And finally, and above all, each form is discovered to be a form of the one object. This is the sense of biblical exegesis, as well as of the stocktaking and analysis known as Church history, or the history of dogmatics and theology. It is likewise the sense of the different loci, chapters, and paragraphs of dogmatics and ethics, as well as of the consideration of the many practical tasks of the Church.

The formation of a system will always be made in passing only; it will remain rudimentary and fragmentary. The difference between the times and situations in which the theological act of knowledge is carried out opposes any thoroughgoing and consistent systematization. Systematization is further opposed by the great variety of the forms and aspects of the single object of theology. And, above all, a system is opposed by the fact that the theological center which comprehends and displays its manifold individual aspects is no blueprint available for the asking. It is, instead, Jesus Christ who, by the potency of the Holy Spirit, is risen, powerful, and speaking. It is the continuously novel binding and liberating goodness of the living God who comes down to man and draws man up to himself in a history that is always freshly in motion. He reigns, and beside him there is no other ruler. There is no systematic power behind the throne. And he is also the one who impedes the appearance of any stagnant nooks in which philosophical or "historical" thought and speech might sometime become possible or even required. He does not allow the theologian to overlook even one point of the circumference; to let any one point stand in some sort of isolation; or to shun thinking it through earnestly and honestly, i.e., theologically. But he also does not allow the theologian to mistake any one point for the center itself, or to create an epicenter competing with the primary center, or to fashion an ellipse out of the circle and in this way succumb to sectarianism, heresy, or perhaps even apostasy. "Everything is yours," but "He who does not gather with me scatters." One of the first criteria of genuine theological knowledge of the *intellectus fidei* is that it gathers "with him." It is a knowledge that gathers all thoughts, concepts, and words to him as their beginning and goal.

2. The object of theology, which is the God of the Gospel in his work and word, is related to the knowledge of God in the same way that God is related to man, the Creator to his creature, and the Lord to his servant. He is in every respect the one who comes first. The knowledge of him can only follow and be subordinated and accommodated to him. He commits, frees, and summons the theologian to notice, consider, and speak of him. The theologian cannot espouse the cause of any a priori that would take precedence over him. According to the rule of Hilary, *Non sermoni res, sed rei sermo subjectus est* (The thing is not subject to the word, but the word is subject to the thing). Or, as the same idea is expressed in Anselm's terms, the *ratio* and the *necessitas* of theological knowledge must be directed by the *ratio* and the *necessitas* of its object. This relationship may not be reversed! Naturally, as a human science, theology constantly and universally employs the viewpoints, concepts, images, and linguistic media that have been handed down or have newly arisen in its time and situation. In this respect it is no different from any other human science. Its knowledge was won in different ways during the last days of antiquity, in the Middle Ages, in the era of the baroque, or during the Enlightenment, in idealism or romanticism. But there is no time or situation in which theology can allow itself to recognize some general regulation as a binding law for its viewpoints, conceptions, images, and speech. And by no means may

theology let itself be bound by any such regulation that rules or desires to rule at the present. It makes no difference whether this regulation is proclaimed in the name of Aristotle, Descartes, Kant, Hegel, or Heidegger.

One reason theology cannot recognize such a law is that a specific philosophy and world view usually stand behind every such regulation. Theology would necessarily have to tolerate such conceptions, to the detriment of the pursuance of its task. But the primary reason it cannot bow to such a regulation is that it is summoned and commissioned by its object for a sight, thought, and speech that are open and flexible on all sides. It is unconditionally bound to its object alone.

On the other hand, why should theology not also employ current ideas, concepts, images, and expressions? As long as these prove themselves suitable, why could they not be "eclectically" used with the greatest confidence? Such a use definitely would not imply that theology would have to acknowledge as an authoritative precept for itself whatever is in current usage. It must inquire into the logic, dialectic, and rhetoric that stem from its object, the divine Logos. It will have to risk going its own way straight through the domain of those other criteria which have to do with the ideas, thought, and speech that are considered at present to be generally valid or are more or less solemnly proclaimed abroad. Progress and improvement in theology are never to be expected from obsequious obedience to the spirit of the age; they can stem only from increased determination to pursue the law of theological knowledge itself, even when theologies are maintaining a cheerful openness toward the spirit of the times.

We recall what was said in the first lecture about the character of theology as a *free* science. It preserves its freedom by making use of every human capacity for perception, judgment, and speech, without being bound to any presupposed epistemology. At this point it opposes not only the older orthodoxy but also every modern neo-orthodoxy. In its free and eclectic use of human capacities it pursues but one thing, that is, to render the obedience which is demanded of it by its object, the living God in the living Jesus Christ and in the Holy Spirit's power of life. It is not called to irrationality, to lazy or fanciful thought, and certainly not to a perverse love of the paradoxical as such. *Credo quia absurdum* (I believe because it is absurd) would be the last thing to profit its object or to be permitted theology. On the contrary, the theologian cannot possess, maintain, and demonstrate enough reason. However, the object of his science has a way of its own for laying claim to his reason. This way is often familiar, but also often quite unfamiliar. This object is not bound to set its standards by the little theologian. The little theologian, however, is certainly committed to setting his standards by it. This priority of the object over its apperception is the second important criterion of genuine theological knowledge, the *intellectus fidei*.

3. The object of theology, the work and word of God in the history of Immanuel and its biblical testimony, has a definite propensity, a definite emphasis and tendency, an irreversible direction. The theologian is committed, freed, and summoned to give room to this emphasis in his knowledge, the *intellectus fidei*. There is a double aspect in God's action and speech and, correspondingly, in the texts of the Old and New Testaments (which only apparently stand alongside one another with equal weight!). This double aspect may be signified as the divine Yes and No energetically spoken to man, or as the Gospel lifting man up and the Law setting him aright, as the grace directed to him and the condemnation threatening him, or as the life for which he has been saved and the death to which he is subjected. To

be faithful to the Word of God and the scriptural testimony witnessing to that Word, the theologian must visualize, consider, and speak of both aspects, the light as well as the shadow. But with the same faithfulness he cannot mistake, deny, or conceal the fact that both of these moments are not related to one another like the movements of a pendulum, constantly repeated with equal force in opposite directions, or like balance scales equally weighted and indecisively oscillating. Their relationship, instead, is like a before and after, an above and a below, a more and a less. There is no mistaking the fact that here man is made to hear a sharp and overwhelming divine No. But there is also no mistaking the fact that this No is enclosed within God's creative, reconciling, and redeeming Yes to man. The Law that binds man is certainly established and proclaimed here, but its divine validity and divinely binding power are due no less certainly to its character as the Law of the covenant and as a form of the Gospel. A condemnation is undoubtedly pronounced and executed at this juncture, but in this very condemnation reconciling grace is clearly displayed, as in the decisive execution of this condemnation on the Cross at Golgotha. Death appears here unmistakably as the final boundary of every human beginning and end, but man's eternal life also unmistakably appears as the meaning and goal of his death.

God's Yes and No are not ambivalent. Gospel and Law do not possess a complementary character. There is no balance, rather there is the greatest imbalance. Just such superiority on the one hand and inferiority on the other are what theology must adequately express in the double aspect of God's relation to man. Although it definitely may not reduce what God wills, does, and says to a triumphal Yes to man, it may also not let matters stand by a No that with equal authority and weight match God's Yes. Any precedence of God's No over his Yes

(not to speak of a disappearance of his Yes in his No
so that, in short, the light would be set in shadow instead
of what is shadowy being brought into the light) is
altogether out of the question. Romans 7 may neither
explicitly nor implicitly become more familiar, important, and dear to the theologian than Romans 8, just as
hell may not become more indispensable and interesting than heaven. Similarly, in Church history, to point
out the sins, faults, and weaknesses of the scholastics
and the mystics, Reformers and Papists, Lutherans and
Reformed, rationalists and pietists, orthodox and liber-
als—even though these failings certainly dare not be
overlooked or left unmentioned—cannot become a more
urgent task than seeing and understanding them all in
the light of the forgiveness of sins that is necessary and
promised to us all. Lastly, the theologian may not be
more agitated by the godlessness of the children of this
world than by the sun of righteousness which has already arisen upon them as well as upon himself.

In the first lecture we called theology a happy science.
Why are there so many really woeful theologians who
go around with faces that are eternally troubled or even
embittered, always in a rush to bring forward their
critical reservations and negations? The reason is their
lack of respect for this third criterion of genuine theological knowledge. They do not respect the internal
order of the theological object, the superiority of God's
Yes over his No, the Gospel over the Law, of grace over
condemnation, and life over death, but instead they wish
arbitrarily to transmute this into an equilibrium or even
to reverse the relationship. No wonder they come into
unhappy proximity to the older J. J. Rousseau or also to
that pitiable man (whom Goethe memorialized in his
Winter Trip Through the Harz) requesting comfort
from the "Father of love." A theologian may and should
be a pleased or satisfied man, if not always on the sur-

face then all the same deep within. To be "satisfied" in the good old sense of this word means to have found sufficiency in something. As Paul Gerhardt says in one of his hymns: "Let this suffice you, and be still in the God of your life."* If anyone should not find it sufficient to be "in God," what sufficiency would he find in the community or world? How could he exist as a theologian? The community knows from experience that it is a lost flock, but it does not know, or never knows adequately, that it is God's beloved and chosen people, called as such to praise him. And the world knows from experience that it lies in the power of evil (no matter how much it may continually delude itself about its predicament). But it does not know that it is upheld on all sides by the helping hands of God. The theologian finds satisfaction when his knowledge, the *intellectus fidei,* is directed by the thrust conveyed to him by the object of his science. In this way he becomes and remains a satisfied and pleased man, who also spreads satisfaction and pleasure throughout the community and world.

* First line of a hymn by Paul Gerhardt, 1666.

In our answer to the question of what makes a man a theologian we have reached a point where a momentary pause is necessary. We must now look in quite a different direction in order properly to understand what we have said about this subject. There was no particular difficulty in making fairly comprehensible and clear what was involved in wonderment, concern, and commitment, those phenomena which are based on the object of theological science and which assault those who are occupied with this science. But can we make clear how this assault occurs? Can we make clear how someone, as a result, becomes, remains, and always newly again becomes such an astonished, concerned, and committed man? To do this we must first underscore one aspect of our discussion of commitment. Granted that the character of the knowledge to which the theologian is *committed*, freed, and summoned is indeed special. How, then, does it happen that someone becomes really and effectively committed to this knowledge and its very special direction? How does someone begin to move along the path shown him by the object of theological science? With this as a point of departure, a further question certainly can and must be posed in retrospect. How does someone become seriously *concerned* by this object, or how is he even filled with serious *wonderment?* What is the genesis of these phenomena?

Obviously we now find ourselves in quite a similar situation (or basically no doubt the same one) as in our fifth lecture on the Spirit. There we were obliged to admit the lack of presuppositions for our earlier statements regarding the Word of God, its biblical witnesses, and the community founded by those witnesses. Now, once again, we confront a discontinuity which is rooted in the matter itself. We can neither overlook nor make light of this discontinuity, nor can we attempt to do away with it by argumentation, least of all by bringing in some sort of *Deus ex machina.* Nothing here can be presupposed! Just as before, all that can be required (and allowed) is the indication of a factor which cannot be built into any system. Just as before, we must meditate on the free Spirit as the mystery of the Word of God which was heard and attested to by the prophets and apostles and which founds, sustains, and rules the community. And also as before, we must renounce any systematic control, and point simply to an event which takes place in divine and human freedom. Although without presuppositions, inconceivable and inexplicable, this event is all the same describable. In it the object of theology claims, astonishes, concerns, and commits any given man in such a way that he can actually live, inquire, think, speak, and totally exist as a theologian. This event is *faith,* the little bit of faith of a definitely very little man.

The first thing called for is, appropriately, a few delimitations of the concept of faith, so battered in older and especially in recent Protestantism.

Firstly, faith would no doubt be a somewhat petty event, scarcely worth mentioning in this context, if what was meant by it was a human notion. Having reached the boundary of what he considers to be certain human knowledge, a man might allow room for a suspicion or opinion, the posing of a postulate, or the application of a calculus of probability. He might then equate the object of theology with what he suspects, postulates, or considers probable, and, in this sense, affirm the object. All this may, of course, be done, but such a man should not suppose that this is the faith by which he may become and remain a theologian. No one can merely think, suppose, or postulate the object which astonishes, concerns, and commits a man in the sense we have described. Faith in this object, therefore, is not hypothetical and problematic knowledge. It is quite basically a most intensive, strict, and certain knowledge. Compared with it, even what is supposedly the most certain knowledge on our side of the human boundary can only be esteemed a hypothesis—perhaps useful, but fundamentally beset by problems.

Secondly, it would also be an inadequate faith if someone were to assent to certain propositions and doctrines relating to the object of theology by appropriating such formulations on the basis of their own authority. He might have encountered such formulations at second hand, perhaps through some major or minor witnesses to the Word of God whom he deems exemplary, or through the dogma and confession of the Church, or even through the Bible. He assumes that he himself knows what those others apparently knew (although in reality he does not know this at all). This is the procedure which Wilhelm Herrmann untiringly, irreconcilably, and (for his hearers) unforgettably pilloried at the beginning of our century as the most unpardonable of all sins. Certainly it is a wretched retreat from the quest for truth. Certainly such a decision and its fulfillment on the basis of blind faith smack of a *sacrificium intellectus* and not of *fides quaerens intellectum,* of disbelief and not of belief. Certainly *fides implicita* is a despicable concept of a despicable matter, which should never in any way have been adorned with the name of *fides.* Certainly a house of cards is constructed here in which no one would be well advised to take occupancy as a Christian and as a theologian.

Another and third concept of faith, instead of being inadequate, is rather too magnificent and audacious.

Indeed, someone might fancy that with his bit of faith he actually experienced and achieved a representation of the incarnation (with or without sacramental reassurances), or in a miniature version, of the faith of Jesus. He might suppose himself appointed and able to set divinity in motion in his life, or possibly to create it, according to the rule *fides creatrix divinitatis in nobis* (faith is the creator of divinity in us). Such presumptuous faith might befit a pious Hindu, *mutatis mutandis,* but it should not represent itself as Christian faith. Christian faith occurs in the *encounter* of the believer with him in whom he believes. It consists in communion, not in identification, with him.

Fourthly, it was never a desirable tendency to exalt faith into an ontic and central concept, displacing the real object of theology, as though faith were the theme and the true event of salvation. This is what has happened to a wide extent in modern Protestantism, which excessively emphasizes the desire to understand and pursue theology as *pisteology,* the science and doctrine of Christian faith. The Bible and Church history are then searched exclusively and decisively for witnesses and, if possible, heroes of faith. Everything that might be worth considering with respect to God's work and word is accepted only as a thought or expression of faith, or reinterpreted as such, and whatever does not seem to submit to this treatment, is excised either tacitly or with express disqualifications. As if the word *credo,* as such, were the real confession in the Credo of the Church! As if man were called to believe and confess, not God the Father, Son, and Holy Spirit, but the faith of the Church which expresses itself first in these high-flown words, and finally in his very own faith! (Unfortunately, there is also a Mozart mass, known as the *Credo Mass,* which might lead to this misunderstanding, since its *credo* is penetratingly repeated throughout all three of its articles.)

Faith is the *conditio sine qua non*, the indispensable condition of theological science, but not its object and theme. How could it ever be its central theme? The real object of theology certainly demands faith, but it also opposes any attempt to dissolve it into thoughts and expressions of faith. Whoever does not recognize this should not be surprised by the fruitless labor that theological endeavor must then have in store for him.

Faith is the *conditio sine qua non* of theological science! This is to say, faith is the event and history without which no one can become and be a Christian. Without this event a man may be characterized by all sorts of other worth-while capabilities and qualities, but he cannot become and be a theologian. Actually we have already spoken about this root of theological existence in the previous three lectures; however, we were only able to speak of wonder, concern, and commitment in the form of descriptions of an *event*.

Faith is the special event that is constitutive for both Christian and theological existence. Faith is the event by which the wonderment, concern, and commitment that make the theologian a theologian are distinguished from all other occurrences which, in their own way, might be noteworthy and memorable or might be given the same designation.

What happens in the event of faith is that the Word of God frees one man among many for faith itself. This is the motivation of faith; something is "moved," and something really "takes" place. By God's Word, together with the life-giving power and the unique sovereignty of the Spirit, one man among many is permitted to exist continually as a free man. He is freed to affirm this Word as something not only thoroughly comforting and helpful, but also binding and indisputably valid for the world, the community, and finally for himself. He is freed to put his whole joyful trust in this Word and to become unreservedly obedient to what this announcement of God himself expresses about his love for the world, his people, and also for the theologian. No one can take such action by his own power. A man can do this only when he is overcome by God's Word and its Spirit of power; when he is resurrected and recreated by it for such an act. But along with this origin in God's free Word and the direction toward this Word, this act is genuinely and freely man's *own*. The one who affirms, trusts, and obeys is not, as it were, God in him, but he himself, this little man. Also, the events of affirmation, trust, and obedience exclude the idea that man might be acting in some sort of enthusiastic delirium. No. He believes, receives, and follows God and his Word as a man, by the enlistment and use of his normal human understanding (although not leaving out his human fantasy!), his human will, and no doubt also his human feeling. But although humanly determined and limited, he does this as a free man, as a man who he *was not* but nevertheless *became* when encountered by God's Word spoken in his work. Although strictly speaking he "is" not this man, he is allowed to become this man again and again when this object finds and confronts him anew, enabling and requiring him to affirm, trust, and obey itself. When that happens to someone, and when someone does that, he believes. And when this event, as such, is revelatory and this deed, as such, is enlightened, faith has the fundamental character of knowledge. As the *intellectus fidei*, it is knowledge of its object—that object which is the very origin of faith. From this origin and object, faith receives its concrete and distinctive content and is allowed to become knowledge of God and man, of the covenant of God with man, and of Jesus Christ. Certainly this is not only an intellectual knowledge, but what interests us here is that it is *also* knowledge executed in concepts and spoken in words. Faith is allowed to reoccur repeatedly when it is *fides quaerens intellectum,* faith laboring quite modestly, but not fruitlessly, in the quest for truth. This is the way the object of theology lays claim to a man, allowing him to perceive, inquire, think, and even speak theologically. This process remains inconceivable and inexplicable (and here we think of what was said in the sixth lecture about the miracle of theological existence as such). But it is nevertheless capable of being described, since it involves the healing of one who was previously blind, deaf, and dumb, but who now sees, hears, and speaks.

It remains for us now to observe a few special emphases:

1. The statement has often been made that one must believe in order to become and be a theologian. This expression is correct insofar as a person who is not freed for faith will not be able to hear, see, or speak theologically, but will only display a splendid triviality in every theological discipline. But to say that a person *must* believe would be inappropriate, since he can only really believe as a *free* believer, as one freed for faith. The same applies to Schiller's statement, "You must believe, you must venture, for the gods give no guarantees." Such a thoroughly heathen wisdom is inapplicable to Christian faith. First of all, faith is definitely no such venture as that which Satan, for instance, suggested to the Lord on the pinnacle of the temple (Luke 4:9–12). It is, instead, a sober as well as a brave appropriation of a firm and certain promise. Secondly, this appropriation definitely never occurs without the possession of a very real guarantee in the presence and action of the Spirit who, at least in the opinion of the Apostle Paul, frees man for faith. And finally, this act is not a necessity but a per-

mission granted man by God, consisting in the natural sequence and response by which man returns a bit of human gratitude for the grace shown him by God. Such faith is comparable to the natural development of a bud into a flower and the natural inclination of this flower toward the sun, or to the natural laughter of a child when he beholds something that gives him pleasure.

2. Faith is a history, new every morning. It is no state or attribute. It should not be confused with mere capacity and willingness to believe. Of course, it may result in and involve all sorts of faithfully held convictions, which had better be called the sum of some sort of "insight." Faith might, indeed, include the insight, let us say, that the theologian would do well not to throw up his hands in disgust and hurriedly pass over to demythologizing procedures when he is confronted, for instance, by affirmations regarding Jesus' birth from a virgin and his descent into hell, or by the resurrection of the flesh and the report of the empty tomb, or by the trinitarian dogma of Nicea and the Christological dogma of Chalcedon, and perhaps also by the incorporation of the Church into the profession of faith in the Holy Spirit. The theologian might, instead, do well to ask himself seriously whether he really believes—as he supposes he does—in the God of the Gospel when he thinks he can overlook, delete, or reinterpret these and similar points. It might be quite another God in whom he would then actually believe. All the same, willingness to believe all those and similar points is not yet faith. Faith is no *credere quod,* but rather a *credere in,* according to the unmistakable formulation of the Apostles' Creed; it is not a belief "that . . ." but a faith "in . . ."—in God himself, the God of the Gospel who is Father, Son, and Spirit. Whoever believes in him will hardly be able to avoid for any length of time the knowledge of many other points in addition to those we have

cited. Yet faith is not a matter of being full of "belief" in and on such special issues. Instead, what is important is believing in him, God himself, the subject of all predicates. That is what may happen anew every morning *fide quaerente intellectum*, by the faith that seeks knowledge.

3. The criterion of the genuineness and enduring capacity of the faith which is indispensable to the theologian is not its special strength, depth, or fervor. It does not matter that this faith will, as a rule, be rather weak and delicate, fluttering in the windy currents of life and its accidents. If, according to the Gospel, a faith of as mean appearance as a mustard seed is sufficient to move a mountain, it will also be sufficient, not only to make possible, but also to set in motion a fruitful knowledge of God and the theological enterprise. A man is capable of knowledge and theological existence when, along with his bit of faith whose power in this affair avails to nothing, he remains directed and continually redirects himself toward the one *in whom* he may believe. He is a man free for this belief because he has been freed.

4. "I hear the message well enough, but what I lack is faith," said Goethe's Faust.* Yes, indeed—who does *not* lack faith? Who *can* believe? Certainly no one would believe if he maintained that he "had" faith, so that nothing was lacking to him, and that he "could" believe. Whoever believes, knows and confesses that he cannot "by his own understanding and power"** in any way believe. He will simply *perform* this believing, without losing sight of the unbelief that continually accompanies him and makes itself felt. Called and illumined by the Holy Spirit as he is, he does not understand himself; he cannot help but completely wonder at himself. He will

* From Goethe's *Faust*, Part One (scene "Night").
** From Luther's *Smaller Catechism*, Third Article, 1531.

say "I believe" only in and with the entreaty, "Lord, help my unbelief." For this very reason he will not suppose that he *has* his faith, but he will hope and hope and hope for it as the Israelites hoped afresh every morning for the manna in the wilderness. And when he receives this faith afresh, he will also daily activate it anew. For this reason the question whether faith or the event of faith lies within anyone's domain is a frivolous question. The event of faith lies in no one's domain. The serious question, however, is whether anyone can allow himself to persist in the dreary assertion, "What I lack is faith," once he has been shown that and how God's work is done, God's word is spoken, and God's Spirit is operating in the word in which man lives. Or will he leave off all coquetry with his own unbelief and live in the freedom that has been revealed and granted to him? Will he be a man who is not only willing but is also able to take part in the *intellectus fidei* and theological science? Will he be a man who is really and effectively astonished, concerned, and committed by the living God—and who thus is fitted for this undertaking?

III THE THREAT TO THEOLOGY

As we approach this third sequence of reflections, a certain darkening of the scene is inevitable. The undertaking of theology is exposed, from its very beginning and in all its subsequent activities and ramifications, to great threat. An introduction to evangelical theology necessarily involves taking account of this danger; it does so circumspectly and without unnecessary solemnity, but still with complete frankness. There is a good reason for the fact that our designation of theology as a "happy science" seems to stand in such great disharmony with the usual course of theological existence or, at any rate, seems not to be a self-evident attribute of theology. A great deal of theology has an uneasy, insecure, and troubled relationship to its subject; and it can hide its profound, if not bottomless, uneasiness only with difficulty and often with meager success. Naturally, this should not be the case; however, there is a cause for it, which lies not only in the personal failings of the theologian but even in the subject itself. Though this is a good and, properly understood, the best subject with which a man can concern himself, the fact cannot be denied or suppressed that involvement in theology is involvement in a difficult situation. The theologian's difficulty is so great that we can thoroughly understand, even if we must regret, Faust's complaint that, along with many other sciences, he had *"unfortunately* also studied theology with genuine and fervent industry."

What must be spoken of now is the uncertainty which assails theology and the theologian—the very same theologian who, according to our earlier statements, is astonished, concerned, committed, and summoned to faith. This uncertainty is not absolute, but despite its relativity it is very penetrating. The several selected minor chords will no doubt pass over finally and conclusively into a subdued major key. Nevertheless, because there is no escaping this uncertainty, it must *also* be discussed.

Whoever takes up the subject of theology discovers himself immediately, recurrently, and inevitably banished into a strange and notoriously oppressive solitude.

In our old church hymnal we used to sing with emotion a song by Novalis containing the line, "Be content to let others wander in their broad, resplendent, teeming streets." These words might sound very appropriate as a slogan for theology; however, they would not be altogether honest, for who at bottom would not really like to be an individual in a *greater* crowd? Who, as long as he is not the oddest of odd fellows, would not like to have his work supported by the direct or at least indirect acknowledgment and participation of the general public, and understood by all men or at least as many as possible? As a rule, the theologian will have to put up with pursuing his subject in a certain isolation, not only in the so-called "world," but also in the Church (and behind a "Chinese wall," as will soon enough be said). To make this clear, we need only consider how the *venerabilis ordo Theologorum,* the venerable order of divines, usually exists not only as the most delicate but also as the most spectacularly tiny department in most of our universities. At any rate, it ranks numerically as an outsider and is set in the shadows by its far more stately sisters. We might think, above all, of the especially pathetic figure of the pastor in his solitude—his solitary pathway and the uncanny isolation, which, due to the priestly halo which he is still thought to wear, continue to characterize him. He remains a stranger among all the men of his urban or rural community; at best he may be surrounded by a small circle of those who feel particularly concerned. Scarcely anyone (with the exception of one or another colleague who is not geographically or doctrinally too remote from him) can offer him a helping hand in the labor demanded of him, in the explication and application of the biblical message, and in his own theological work.

We might think of the relationship, strange even in a quantitative way, between what has to be said to human beings during the course of an hour in Church preaching and teaching (if they are willing and able to hear it) and what is brought home to them in an unbroken flood by the newspapers, radio, and television. And these are only symptoms of the isolation of the theological concern, task, and effort, an isolation that repeatedly breaks through all opposing interpretations, gestures, and endeavors (despite the ridiculous phrase about "the Church's claim to free speech"). This isolation must be endured and borne, and it cannot always be easily borne with dignity and cheerfulness.

Such isolation is hard to bear because fundamentally it seems *not* to correspond to the essence of theology. Indeed, to assume a theological post in some remote place from which the public is all but excluded seems strikingly to contradict the character of theology. Religion may be a private affair, but the work and word of God are the reconciliation of the *world* with God, as it was performed in Jesus Christ. The object of theology, therefore, is the most radical change of the situation of all humanity; it is the revelation of this change which affects all men. In itself, revelation is undoubtedly the affair of the general public in the most comprehensive sense. What it has spoken into human ears demands proclamation from the housetops.

Must it not be said, however, in the opposite direction, that the essential character of other human sciences does not equip them to consider theology simply as one among themselves? Can other sciences really keep theology separated from themselves, isolated in some corner like a merely tolerated Cinderella? Should not the object of theology be a prototype and pattern for the originality and authority of the objects that occupy the attention of all sciences? Should not general scientific thought and speech find a prototype and pattern in the primacy that theology grants to the rationale of its object above all the principles of its own human knowledge? Can the particularity of theology among all other sciences be understood except by the requirement made of theology: that it, at any rate, dare not fail at the point where other disciplines seem to fail? Can theology be called to do anything other than to offer itself as a stopgap for the other sciences? Is not all science, as such, basically called to be theology and to make the special science of theology superfluous? Should not the isolated existence of theology be understood as an abnormal fact when judged by the nature of theology, as well as by that of the other sciences? Must not even the peculiarity of theological existence, as such, be designated, both initially and ultimately, as an incongruous situation? Should not the attempt be understandable (at least as to its intention) which Paul Tillich has so impressively undertaken in our day: to integrate theology with the rest of the sciences or with culture itself as represented by philosophy and, vice versa, to set culture, philosophy, and other sciences in an indissoluble correlation with theology, according to the scheme of question and answer? Should not the duality of heteronomous and autonomous thinking be supplanted by the unity of theonomous thought? If only the philosopher, as such, wanted to be also a theologian! If only, above all, the theologian, as such, wished to be also a philosopher! According to Tillich, he should and can desire to be this. What solutions! What prospects! "Would that we were there!"*

This and similar attempts to do away with the solitude of theology cannot possibly, however, be carried to completion, for they are based on impossible presuppositions. Every such attempt supposes it can understand and comport itself as either paradisiac, or perfected, or divine theology. It considers itself to be *paradisiac* in a bold resumption of the state before the fall; *perfected* in a bold presumption that transcends the time still remaining between the first and second coming of Jesus Christ; or *divine* and *archetypal* in a bold assumption rejecting the distinction between Creator and creature. A theology that was still sinless or already perfected, not to speak of God's very own theology, could self-evidently only be *the* philosophy and *the* science. It could not be a special science distinct from philosophy or the rest of the sciences, and still less could it be relegated to a dusty corner by these. It would be *the* philosophy either because the light of God illuminates it, or because it is identical with this light. However, all that men may here and now know and undertake is *human* theology. As such, it can be neither paradisiac (for we are no longer there), nor perfected (for we are not yet there), nor by any means divine (for we will *never* be gods). It can be only a *theologia ektypa viatorum,* theology typical not of God but of man—that is, of men who are pilgrims. It characterizes these men as laborers who, although still blinded, are already enlightened with knowledge through the grace of God, but who nevertheless do not yet view the glory of the coming universal revelation.

If ever there was a pure fantasy, really "too beautiful to be true," it would be the idea of a philosophical theology or a theological philosophy in which the attempt

* Refrain from a German Christmas hymn based on *In dulci jubilo.*

would be made to reason "theonomously." Such wishful thinking would try by means of a correlative integration of concepts to do away with a distinction. A unity would be formed out of the duality which exists either *de iure* (as between divine and human knowledge) or at least *de facto* (as between knowledge that is original and ultimate and that which is present and human). But realism at this point demands the renunciation of such syntheses, notwithstanding the vision of the unity of all sciences in God or of the unity of the origin and goal of their study. Syntheses have small worth because they are too cheaply achieved when there is but a minimum of intellectual talent and will to synthesize. But when he thinks realistically, the theologian will stick to the fact that the *theologia archetypa* and the *theologia ektypa*, as well as the *theologia paradisiaca,* or *comprehensorum,* and the *theologia viatorum,* are two different things, and that his problem and task can only be the latter, not the former, of these concepts.

Things would have gone differently and more favorably for the history of modern theology if the foregoing distinctions, which are only apparently abstruse, had not become, at the ominous turn of the seventeenth century, a part of "dogmatic antiquity" (according to Karl von Hase). Of course, one may complain about the limited viewpoint displayed in them or look with longing and hope beyond them toward the perfected theology. But the theologian must still carefully avoid trying to produce from his own resources that perfection. Instead, he must simply recognize that what is apparently abnormal is really the normal for this day and age.

Theological knowledge, thought, and speech cannot become general truths, and general knowledge cannot become theological truth. Distressing as the situation may be, there is no getting around the special character and relative solitude of theology in relation to other sciences.

Is this not also the situation of the community which is summoned to attest to the work and word of God in the world in which theology must perform its task? If this people of God, wandering between the times, does not wish to betray its calling, it can only proclaim the work and word of God to its environment as a supremely novel event. It will not try to integrate its knowledge of this novelty with the different knowledge of its environment or, in reverse order, the different knowledge of its environment with its own knowledge. Theology will not be ashamed of the solitude in which the community of the last days finds itself placed by the execution of its missionary charge. Rather, theology will, in its own solitude, partake in the solitude of the community—whether this happens with sighs or with smiles shining through tears. It dare not try to break free of its solitude. The community must endure and bear its isolation with dignity and cheerfulness; it will endure and bear its solitude as a form of the threat and risk that do not adhere to it by chance alone.

The inexplicable solitude of theology and the theologian has definite consequences. Often enough the theologian will experience visible proofs or justifications for his feeling that he stands *alone* in this calling. He alone seems involved in what we described in the second series of these lectures as the wonderment, concern, and commitment that make a man a theologian. Even in the community and, worst of all, among all too many of his fellow theologians, the theologian seems to stand and persevere alone. Perhaps he is not so completely alone as he, at especially troubled moments, may assume! The fact that he is not suffering private hallucinations, as he occasionally imagines, can suddenly become clear to him even in the statements of men who do not seem to be Christians at all. Although they would radically reject the notion or claim that they were theologians, they seem actually to know the violent disturbance that makes him a theologian. Of course, he cannot count on their support. *Intra et extra muros ecclesiae,* inside and outside the walls of the Church, he will, in fact, often enough cast about in vain for companions who are also filled with wonder, who are also concerned and committed. Instead of finding support, he will often receive the painful impression that innumerable Christians and non-Christians apparently find it quite easy to withdraw more or less unscathed from the shock that makes one a theologian. (I know two men, both doctors and excellent men after their fashion, who cordially but definitely consider the mental state of the theologian to be at best a type of sickness—which is probably inherited! How could such a view not help but make the theologian insecure and appear, not only as a menace to his own existence, but as a manifestation of the danger of all theology as such?)

What does not seem to be every man's possession at this point is *faith* itself. Faith is the fundamental relationship by which the violent disturbance of theology is distinguished from other exciting human experiences. Of course, the faith of the Christian *community* is the real thing which makes a man a theologian. Faith is the use of the freedom which is granted corporately to all Christians, by which they may affirm the Word of God, put all their trust in him, and obey him wholly. Thus the theologian seems to have no lack of "companions in faith." But the Christian community, as the *congregatio fidelium,* is a congregation of men who are characterized by the fact that *each one* (if he really does believe) is so compelled and willing to believe that he would believe even if he were the *only* believing man in the whole world. There is no other way to exist as a theologian. There is no other way such a man can carry out his particular function in the community and the world. And he faces a hard trial when, now and again, he is put to the proof concerning this solitude that is necessary precisely for the sake of the community in *faith*. And he also faces a hard trial when a continual demonstration is required of the latent truth that no one else can take his place when it comes to faith and his participation in the faith of the community. At his side he will surely find a few companions, and only of these few can he be moderately sure.

How, then, can he ever be sure of his own faith? Are not his faith, his theological existence, and theology, as such, called into question by this solitude—however much they are guaranteed by the Word of God and the *testimonium Spiritus Sancti*, the testimony of the Holy Spirit? In this quandary Calvin and, before him, Augustine and others reached out for the sternest form of the doctrine of predestination. But even this information cannot yield an effective solace for one who is solitary. There was actually nothing left for Calvin to do but to endure and bear the very solitude of his faith, in order in this very way to think and speak as a theologian eminently bound to the Church.

The real cause, however, for the loneliness of the man concerned with theology is the special theological thinking that is invariably demanded of him. What leads him again and again into solitude is precisely the special character of the *intellectus fidei*. How could there be, even among those who have been freed for faith, a great many men ready and able to appropriate the sole possible method for the performance of the *intellectus fidei*? How should very many ever be willing to make the turn of 180 degrees that is required, not just once, but every day anew? How should a crowd be able to question and reply, not from the viewpoint of men, but on the basis of God's Word spoken to men? No wonder that in and outside of the community of the faithful, most men think that adoption of this method, the completion of this turn, and the exclusive obedience to God's Word are too rigid for them and demand to much of them. No wonder that they are inclined to perceive nothing else but an unnatural bondage in the spiritual freedom they are promised! If only these men, moreover, were merely doctors, lawyers, historians, and philosophers, whose disapproval forms the inevitable accompaniment of theology along the way which it is called to go! If only there were not so many men within the theologian's own ranks whom he must observe yearning for the fleshpots of Egypt. Shortly after starting to run (some of them fail utterly to ever get started), these brethren and colleagues advertise themselves as the discoverers of the newest of things, while in reality (much like a cat that is used to landing on its four legs) they are merely relapsing into some sort of psychologism, historism, or, at best, some kind of anthropology, ontology, or linguistics. If the theologian is really concerned about theology, he should not regret having to swim against the stream of fellow theologians and nontheological opinions and methods. If the results of his work are not to be trivialities, he dare not feel sorry about the pain and the cost of enduring a continuous solitude.

Finally, however, theology is not simply exegesis, Church history, and dogmatics. It is ethics as well. Ethics is the scrutiny of a definite conception of the divine command which is implied in and with the divine promise. Ethics seeks to form a clear conception of those actions to be performed in Church and world which are essential to and typical of the obedience of faith. Ethics seems to formulate the practical task assigned to man by the gift of freedom. But an immediate conformity is not to be expected between this conception and the

wishes, attitudes, and efforts that are current and dominant at any one time, both in the world and in the
Church. What is, as a rule, much more to be expected in
this area is a more or less definite opposition between
theology with its questions and answers and the opinions
and principles of Mr. and Mrs. "Everyman," be these
major or minor characters, un-Christian or even Christian. Although theology is no enemy to mankind, at its
core it is a critical, in fact a revolutionary affair, because,
as long as it has not been shackled, its theme is the new
man in the new cosmos. Whoever takes up this theme
must be prepared, precisely because of what he thinks
and says in the *practical* sphere, to displease the masses.
Any environment that measures itself by its own yard-
stick will find the minority view of theology and the
theologian seriously suspect. In such a situation a person may easily become desperate, bitter, skeptical, perhaps even bellicose and mean; he may become inclined,
as an accuser, to turn permanently against his fellow
men on account of their lifelong folly and wickedness.
Precisely this, of course, may not be permitted to happen.

If the ethics of evangelical theology does not wish
to convict itself of falsehood, it must be represented,
for all its definiteness, only by the greatest serenity
and peaceableness. Admittedly, its voice will be that of
the "lonely bird on the housetop,"* resounding pleasingly
only in the ears of a few, and constantly exposed to
the danger of being shot down by the first comer—
a risk that is perhaps not always insignificant. It is
likely that theology will scarcely ever become popular,
as little with the pious as with the children of this
world, precisely because of the ethical and practical
disturbance that issues from it directly and indirectly.
Whoever involves himself in theology, if he does this

* Psalms 102:7

seriously, must be ready and able, in a given situation, to endure and bear loneliness just in respect to his practical ethics.

So much for the threat to theology which comes from solitude.

The second form of the endangering of theology is more threatening than the first because it does not accost theology from the outside, but usually occurs within the work of theology itself, remaining, to a certain extent, immanent within it. This form is *doubt*.

There are two different aspects under which we must consider doubt threatening. The first form differs from the second in that the doubt which occurs here belongs by nature to the whole theological undertaking; as such, something must be done to eliminate its dangerousness. In the second form, however, doubt represents a quite unnatural threat to theology, and over against such doubt the only advice that can be given is the same as we offered with respect to solitude—to endure and to bear!

The first form of doubt, although not without danger, is to a certain extent natural and susceptible to treatment. It results from the necessity laid upon theology to pose the question about truth in faithfulness to its commission and with its eyes fixed on the work and word of God. Theology must constantly inquire anew into the content of the revelation which has occurred in God's action, by which he reconciled the world to himself. It must repeatedly discover afresh the truth and reality of this action and the significance of the divine statement made by it. In this sense doubt springs from the theological necessity of treating the quest for truth as a task that is never completed, that is, instead, set before the theologian time and again.

The theology of the Middle Ages, as well as that of the older Protestantism, was carried on by means simply of "Questions." It was thus characterized by

radical and untiringly inquisitive occupation with the
question about truth. This is obviously not quite in
accord with what John Doe usually thinks of when he
hears the word "orthodoxy." The questions envisaged
by theology, in which even apparently primitive doctrines like the existence of God were placed in doubt,
were posed as precisely as possible. The attempt was
then made in each case to find answers which, as far as
possible, would be just as precise as the questions. The
formulations of the old catechisms likewise followed
the method of the interplay of questions and answers.
Among these the Heidelberg catechism, for example,
could even ask whether the Reformation doctrine of
justification did not produce "careless and crazy people"
—truly a full-blooded doubt! In this sense, doubt simply
marks the fact that nothing in theology is self-evident.
Nothing can be had for nothing. Everything must be
worked through, in order to acquire validity. A paradisiac theology would not need any such work; a theology of glory would also not need it; and in the archetypal theology of God himself, the question about truth
would form a total unity with its answer. But this is
not the case in the *theologia ektypa viatorum* allotted
to us for the time between Easter and the second coming
of Jesus Christ. This period requires theological work,
frank questions, and also ("Socratic") doubt.

"In the sweat of your face you shall eat bread until
you return to the ground, for out of it you were taken."
This is just as valid for every pastor on every Saturday
when he prepares a sermon as it is for every student
who listens to a lecture or reads a book. But not everyone is prepared to expose himself repeatedly to "Socratic" doubt or to let it cost him a little sweat to answer
the question about truth which arises along every step of
the way. In view of the necessity of doubting in order
to move forward toward truth, the sluggard might say

with Proverbs 22 :13, " 'There is a lion outside! I shall be slain in the streets!' " He might give up theological work even before he had begun. The toil involved in this type of altogether necessary and legitimate doubt obviously implies a very serious endangering of theology, for there are many sluggards; indeed, we are all basically sluggards. Nonetheless, this danger can be overcome. *Fiat!* Let it be done!

The case is different in the second form of doubt. There, an uneasiness could, and in fact does, spring up at the very center of the performance of the theological task. The question might arise whether the whole theological enterprise, in general or in particulars, should even be ventured, much less carried out. According to our earlier reflections, it cannot be taken for granted that the quest for truth is posed in any way by God's work and word, or that this quest has been assigned us as a task and, therefore, should at least be wrestled with by us. Even less to be taken for granted is the confidence that the theological endeavor is not only relevant, but that its proper object exists. Is not doubt in the existence of God something always uncannily easy even for someone who long ago saw through the simplicity of such doubt, or who has perhaps learned from Anselm how to handle it in the proper way? Such doubt was already a popular illness among the cultured of the early eighteenth century, and even the famous German pietist Count Zinzendorf seems to have cultivated it in his youth. What, however, would be the consequence if the theologian actually surrendered at the very point at which opposition to such doubt should be marshaled? What if he staggered at the precise moment at which this doubt should actually be seen through and despised as the act of an *insipiens,* the "fool" of Psalm 53? Is the object of theology, even the history of Immanuel, its revelation and human knowledge of it, a real, solid, re-

liable basis upon which to build? Is there really a foundation, deeper than all pious emotions and their corresponding self-assurance, and stronger than the many
more-or-less useful apologetic arguments, that can be
fashioned from historical, psychological, or speculative
considerations? Does God really exist, work, and speak
in the history of Immanuel, of Israel, of the church, of
theology? Is there really something like that inner testimony of the Holy Spirit, by which we are assured of
God's existence, activity, and speech in that history?
What answer could be given to that man of the eighteenth century who dryly maintained that he personally
had never received such a testimony? David Friedrich
Strauss called the doctrine of the *testimonium Spiritus
Sancti internum* (the inner testimony of the Holy Spirit)
the Achilles' heel of the orthodox Protestant system.
What if someone (or perhaps every theologian) were
openly or secretly vulnerable in just this Achilles' heel?
What if he should, in fact, be wounded there repeatedly?

Be it noted that in this sense as well, doubt does not
mean denial or negation. Doubt only means swaying and
staggering between Yes and No. It is only an uncertainty, although such uncertainty can be much worse
than negation itself. In its second form, doubt means
basic uncertainty with respect to the problem of theology as such (not to be confused with the painstaking,
but necessary openness of theological questioning). This
doubt produces at the outset of theological work an embarrassment with respect to the very necessity and
meaning of theological questioning itself. This embarrassment puts into question God's Word itself—
which is yet to be examined for its truth! The embarrassment questions God's very presence and action—
which yet are the basis and motive of theology's inquiry
into God's Logos! This embarrassment concerns the
very freedom to work as a theologian. Am I free for

this work? Or am I perhaps not free for it at all? Swaying and staggering, being uncertain and embarrassed, saying at the very beginning "perhaps, but perhaps not"—what else can all this be but a serious and threatening danger to theology?

Doubt in this second form can, of course, only be a threat to theology during its human performance within the present time of this world. In this second form, human thought is not, as was the first form of doubt, dialectical by natural necessity. In its relation to God's work and word it does not necessarily have to continually pose and answer questions. Instead, in this second form, human thought is also unnatural, diseased by man's original estrangement, and constantly exposed to the corruption and error which arise and follow from a primal error, that is, the presumption to ask, " 'Did God say . . .' " (Gen. 3:1), or to boldly affirm, " 'There is no God' " (Ps. 53:1), or, " 'I am a god' " (Ezek. 28:9). After the time of this world, however, we await a thorough healing of our human thought, we await a power that will render doubt in the problem of theology no longer a problem for us. This healing is quite remote from the profoundly comforting thought that God certainly does not doubt his own existence. As C. F. Gellert writes in a hymn, "Things will be better in heaven, when I am in the choir of the saints." But this doubt *is* a problem for us in the present age, in the time between the times, in which even the Christian, even the theologian, who is certain of God's grace, is a sinful man.

Swaying and staggering, life in uncertainty and embarrassment about our very relationship to God's work and word—this condition corresponds all too closely to the ambivalence in which we here and now totally exist. The only way we can gaze beyond this ambivalence is in the petition, "Thy Kingdom come!" As to particulars, there can be a great variety of differences between the reasons *for* which and the ways *in* which doubt arises and continually endangers theology. All these ways hark back continually to one basic flaw. Although we (both the community and the Christians who are, including theologians, its members) no doubt quite sufficiently partake of the message of our completed liberation for God, we time and again fundamentally neglect to make use of this freedom to exclude doubt. We see, recognize, and know everything, but then once again we see, recognize, and know nothing at all. Theology cannot here and now become a reality without being accompanied by its deeply internal endangering through this contradiction. Its character remains fragmentary, a "knowing in part" (I Cor. 13:12).

At this point a brief reference should be made to three causes and forms of the doubt that threatens, undermines, and divides theology from within.

Firstly, doubt in theology might powerfully arise in the face of the concentration of the principalities and powers which still rein in this age, competing, with apparent seriousness and undoubtedly with disturbing impressiveness, with the work and word of God. What is the godly power of the Gospel, as praised by Paul in Romans 1:16–17, when compared with the powers of the state or the states, or today with the alliances of states that struggle with one another? What is the power of the Gospel compared with the powers of world economics, natural science, and the technology based upon it, the fine or less fine arts, sport and fashion, ideologies old and new, mystic or rationalistic, moral or immoral? Does not man really live by *these* and scarcely or not at all by the Word that proceeds from the mouth of God? Has God really said something superior to all these powers, something which limits and subdues them all? Has he spoken in such a way that man is now unambiguously committed, as well as freed, to think and speak precisely on the basis of this Word? Must the theologian not be blind who would not let himself be impressed, perhaps gradually, perhaps suddenly, perhaps partially, perhaps completely, by those other powers? How can he avoid losing sight of the object of theology, beginning at least to doubt its meaning and possibility, and becoming (according to the Letter of James) like a wave of the sea, driven and tossed by the wind? "Let no such man suppose that he will receive anything from the Lord!" is what is added there. How could such a man receive anything? But what becomes, then, of the question about truth that is posed for him? What becomes of his service in the community and the world? And, incidentally, what becomes of the theologian himself, since it is he who has taken the risk of joining the pilgrimage of God's people, the community of believers?

But in the second place, doubt can also have its cause in the *community* that encircles the theologian, in the feebleness, disunity, and perhaps even the perverseness of the form and proclamation of his own familiar Church. The great crisis of Christian faith, as well as of Christian theology, that arose in the seventeenth century did not have its primary basis in the rise of modern science, for instance, or of the absolute state which later also became religiously indifferent. According to the illuminating hypothesis of Emmanuel Hirsch, this crisis arose prior to all such shocks, simply in the painfully confusing fact of the stable juxtaposition and opposition of three different churches. Sealed officially and demonstratively in the Peace of Westphalia, these three different confessions each represented exclusive claims to revelation which relativized the claims of each. Subsequent acquaintance with the great non-Christian religions of the Near and Far East underlined this relativity still more painfully. But the vision of God's work and word can also be obstructed for the theologian (as well as for each man) by what confronts him as the Church, as ecclesiastical doctrine and order, or as Christendom and Christianity. Concretely present in individual persons or groups of persons, these Christian relativities may, rightly or wrongly, become an offense to him. Have there not been enough crusades, religious wars, persecutions of the Jews, burnings of witches, and trials of heretics, along with all sorts of persistent Christian failures on the questions of slavery, race, war, women's rights, and social justice? Are there not in the Christian community up to this day, astonishingly rigid examples of prejudice and impatience, along with a sea of theological, as well as Christian, arbitrariness, superficiality, inactivity, disorder, and insignificance? Cannot everything become uncertain and regrettable for someone beholding this underside of the Church? Must not such a person at least *doubt* whether the whole enterprise has any importance? Is it not understandable that theology as a whole should become blighted for one who considers what he perceives (or thinks he perceives) to be the subject of theology itself? Very likely such a person neither could nor would confess, any longer, *credo ecclesiam,* I believe in the Church. How, then, should he confess, as the presupposition of happy and fruitful theological work, *credo in unum Deum,* I believe in one God?

But in the third place, everyone should pay close attention to the possibility that what basically makes himself a doubter is not that the world impresses him so much or that the Church impresses him so little, but rather that there is a structural flaw in his own private life which undoubtedly influences the public side of his conduct. It is a notorious fact that no Christian (and likewise no theologian) can altogether rid himself of this flaw. Two contrasting possibilities must be considered here, of which one or the other (and perhaps both, in ideal competition) plays at least a concomitant role alongside the first two sources of theological doubt which we have described.

The first possibility, on the one hand, may be that the man who is called, ready, and able to do theological work may think he should and can live *dualistically,* in the twin kingdoms of public and private life. He lives in the knowledge of faith, but he is prepared to live this obedient faith only within certain limits. Alongside the *intellectus fidei,* he allows himself a *praxis vitae,* a conduct, which is not controlled by faith, a deportment which departs from faith by following chance or laws of its own. Alongside his knowledge of God's work and word, such a man allows himself a secular and trivial will which is, at all events, not bound and directed by God's. Alongside his thought, speech, and acts, which are kept in order by the object of theology, stand those which are either ordered arbitrarily or not ordered at all. In this way he exists from the very outset in a strained relationship to the Holy Spirit who, according to Paul, is intended and desires to bear witness to his spirit (Rom. 8:16). The tension remains, even should he theoretically affirm the word of the spirit. Who is not familiar with such an affirmation? Small wonder that if he confronts himself honestly, he is obliged to recognize and confess himself as the doubter he is, as a theologian lame and limping on one foot. When he only half believes, he cannot expect to know any more than half. He has to be content with swaying and staggering, since at least he does not collapse completely. Nevertheless, there is an unkind statement in the Book of Revelation that the Lord, if he does not find him hot, would rather see him cold, but finding him only lukewarm, he will spew him out of his mouth. What, then, will become of such a man's theology—though, perhaps, in its special bracket it was far from being the worst?

However, the structural flaw in the theologian's personal conduct that compels him to doubt could be just the opposite. In the relationship of man to God's work and word there may exist not only an unhealthy undernourishment but an equally unhealthy overeating. A man perhaps comes from a family and environment in which theology was not only the Alpha and Omega (as the case should be) but also the substitute, which it should not be, for all the other letters of his alphabet. Or, as a novice, he has devoted himself to theology with the incomparable exclusiveness of a first love; and now he lives not only as a theologian in everything, but even entirely as a theologian *alone,* to the elimination of everything else. He has no basic interest in the newspapers, novels, art, history, sport; and so he reveals that basically he has no interest in any man. He is interested only in his theological work and in his theological concern. Who is not acquainted with this situation? Not only are there students and professors of theology who go beyond their calling, but also preachers who live their whole life hermetically sealed off within their congregations. They associate with other men only in an hypertheological way. A dangerous business! The saying in Ecclesiastes 7:16 is not in vain: "Be not righteous overmuch, and do not make yourself overwise; why should you destroy yourself?" In this way a person can, in fact, destroy himself as a theologian. The reason for this is not merely the great probability that such a person will fail in carrying out his experiment and will then inadvertently and without admitting it succumb once again, and perhaps quite thoroughly, to the syndrome of the two kingdoms and all its corollaries. The major reason is that, like all hypertrophy, theological overemphasis demonstrably leads all too easily to satiety, in this case to what was called in the ancient monastic language the mortal sin of *taedium spirituale,* the spiritual boredom, from which only a small step is needed to arrive at skepticism. *Concentrated* theological work is a good thing, or even the best thing, but *exclusive* theological existence is *not* a good thing. Such existence, in which a man actually plays the deadly role of a God unconcerned about his creation, must sooner or later inevitably lead to doubt, in fact to radical doubt.

We must be content, in conclusion, with three provisional aphorisms concerning doubt:

1. No theologian, whether young or old, pious or less pious, tested or untested, should have any doubt that for some reason or other and in some way or other he is *also* a doubter. To be exact, he is a doubter of the second unnatural species, and he should not doubt that his doubt is by no means conquered. He might just as well— although this would certainly not be "well"—doubt that he is likewise a poor sinner who at the very best has been saved like a brand from the burning.

2. He should also not deny that his doubt, in this second form, is altogether a pernicious companion which has its origin not in the good creation of God but in the *Nihil*—the power of destruction—where not only the foxes and rabbits but also the most varied kinds of demons bid one another "Good night." There is certainly a justification for the doubter. But there is no justification for doubt itself (and I wish someone would whisper that in Paul Tillich's ear). No one, therefore, should account himself particularly truthful, deep, fine, and elegant because of his doubt. No one should flirt with his unbelief or with his doubt. The theologian should only be sincerely *ashamed* of it.

3. But in the face of his doubt, even if it be the most radical, the theologian should not despair. Doubt indeed has its time and place. In the present period no one, not even the theologian, can escape it. But the theologian should not despair; because this age has a boundary

beyond which again and again he may obtain a glimpse
when he begs God, "Thy Kingdom come!" Even within
this boundary, without being able simply to do away
with doubt, he can still offer resistance, at least like the
Huguenot woman who scratched *Résistez!* on the win-
dowpane. Endure and bear it!

So much for the endangering of theology from doubt.

Solitude and doubt do not constitute either the worst or the weightiest threat to theology. Theology may also be called into question by the very object by which it lives, to which it is dedicated, on which its justification is founded, and for whose adequate understanding it labors. It can also be threatened by *God*. It *can?* In fact, it becomes and *is* threatened by him. It finds itself assailed, not only from without (solitude) and not only from within (doubt), but also from above. Its work takes place under conditions of temptation, in a testing by that fire of the righteous and divine wrath which consumes everything of it that is made of wood, hay, and straw (I Cor. 3:12).

The difficult concept of temptation must now be examined. There can be no question but that everything which was reported heretofore about the dangers confronting theology was only child's play compared to what is presently before us.

At the outset it may be wondered why the behavior of so many theologians hardly betrays an awareness of their theology's submission to a test from God. Often, indeed, theology may be seen quite zealously occupied with all sorts of attempts to evade its solitude and to ward off the doubt that undermines it. It seems, however, to suffer remarkably little from fear before the onslaught of God, and it finds astonishingly little reason to meet this gravest and sharpest form of its crisis. But who should not have to wonder, first of all, at himself in this respect? For what theologian could acquit himself of all carelessness in this matter? Who could guarantee, or even boast, that he exists, thinks, and speaks in serious awareness of the divine temptation that confronts his activity? Who could claim to conduct himself or be recognizable as someone who resolutely acknowledges and meets this temptation? On the contrary, the worst thing in this whole sad matter is really the ease with which every theologian fails to notice or repeatedly forgets the fact that his enterprise is threatened by this most radical of endangerments.

The "temptation" encountering theology is simply the event that God withdraws himself from the theological work of man. In this event God hides his face from the activity of the theologian, turns away from him, and denies him the presence and action of his Holy Spirit.

Why should God owe the Holy Spirit to man? Let it not be thought that God's withdrawal is a judgment upon the work of a poor theology only; it can also be a judgment upon the work of a theology that, from a human point of view, is good or even excellent. With respect to the background from which such a theology arises, or regarding the new turn which it is taking, this theology can be outstanding; it may, perhaps, be conservative in the best sense, while at the same time being progressive and up-to-date. Perhaps it has no dearth of biblical and exegetical foundations, or of systematic depth and art, or of actual pointedness and practical usefulness. Perhaps sermons will arise from it which are well prepared and forcefully delivered, and which are readily heard, and justly so, by at least a larger or smaller selected circle of more-or-less modern men. Important literature, with content at once sterling and bold, will be prompted by it, studied, discussed, and tirelessly surpassed by still better works. The young may begin to pay attention, and their elders will be well satisfied. The community appears edified, and the world not disinterested. In short, a gratefully hailed light of the Church is kindled there and appears to shine forth.

Something reflective of this condition of contentment and satiety can be sensed from the inscription which appears under the portrait of an old professor and dean of the Church in Basel (the learned, eloquent, and always satisfied Jerome Burckhardt, who lived at the beginning of the eighteenth century) :

> Make, God, this asset to our town
> Abide for many years.
> He makes Thy holy Word resound
> With vigor in our ears.

So excellent may be the theologian's work. But of what help is it? Everything is in order, but everything is also in the greatest disorder. The mill is turning, but it is empty as it turns. All the sails are hoisted, but no wind fills them to drive the ship. The fountain adorned with many spouts is there, but no water comes. Science there is, but no knowledge illumined by the power of its object. There is no doubt piety, but not the faith which, kindled by God, catches fire. What appears to take place there does not really take place. For what happens is that God, who is supposedly involved in all theological work, maintains silence about what is thought and said in theology *about* him (rather than *of* him as its source and basis). It does happen that the real relation of God to theology and the theologians must be described by a variation of the famous passage in Amos 5: I hate, I despise your lectures and seminars, your sermons, addresses, and Bible studies, and I take no delight in your discussions, meetings, and conventions. For when you display your hermeneutic, dogmatic, ethical, and pastoral bits of wisdom before one another and before me, I have no pleasure in them; I disdain these offerings of your fatted calves. Take away from me the hue and cry that you old men raise with your thick books and you young men with your dissertations!

I will not listen to the melody of your reviews that you compose in your theological magazines, monthlies, and quarterlies.

It is a terrible thing when God keeps silence, and by keeping silence speaks. It is terrible when one or another theologian must notice or, at least, suspect that this occurs, and most terrible of all when many do not even seem to notice and perhaps not even suspect that this occurs. How horrendous it is for them when, pursuing their own carefree way, they fail to notice that theology and all its questions are called in question totally and radically by God. All theology is threatened finally and definitively by the temptation that comes from *him!*

But how can this happen? How can God be absent where such good work takes place, where there is so much concentrated reflection upon him and so much careful respect for his direction, where he is spoken of so expressly, loudly, and earnestly, as is at least attempted in theology? How can God be *against* those who are *for* him? How can he speak the terrible language of silence to those who, like the theologians, would like to behave as his friends? Should God not be a helper, witness, and guarantor when men are obviously concerned with his work and word; and, in the last analysis, not arbitrarily concerned, but concerned according to his call and command? Should he not be present when men have taken up at his command the task of the science of his Logos?

The first thing to be said in reply is that God does not *have* to do anything at all; therefore, he does not have to be present. What happens in the temptation of theology *can* happen. Theologians, even if they are incomparably good and faithful, are still men; in fact, they are sinful men, who not only have no claim to God's assent and support, but must depend upon his free grace to live. One thing holds true in every case of the theologian's work and word: "When thou hidest thy face, they are dismayed; when thou takest away their breath, they die and return to their dust" (Ps. 104:29). God would not be God if he were not free to conduct himself in this manner toward them, letting death be also the wages of their sin. And nothing monstrous occurs when he also makes use of this freedom in relation to them.

But God is not capricious and arbitrary. For all he does, there is good reason. He exercises law and justice when he makes the theologians, the church, and the world realize that even the best theology is in itself and, as such, a *human* work, sinful, imperfect, in fact corrupt and subject to the powers of destruction. It is God's right to show that, in itself, this work is wholly incapable of service to God and his community in the world. Only by God's mercy can it become and remain fitting and useful. God's mercy is the election in which God also rejects; God's calling in which he also discharges and deposes; God's grace in which he also judges; God's Yes which also utters his No. And God's rejection, deposition, judgment, and negation strike, punish, and overturn the very foundations of everything which proves to be continually sinful, imperfect, corrupt, and subject to the power of nothingness—even in man's best works and in man's best theology.

All theological work can only become and be fitting and useful before God and men when it is repeatedly exposed to and obliged to pass through this testing fire. This is the fire of the divine love, but it is also a consuming fire. All that makes theological work pleasing to God and beneficial for the world is what remains of gold, silver, and precious stones, according to I Corinthians 3:12. The passage of theology through this fire is its temptation. Compared to this, even its most desperate solitude or its most radical doubt is only child's play, for what might remain of theology after this fire? The theologian can only have God *for* himself when he has him continually *against* himself. And only when he reconciles himself to this can he, for his part, also desire to be *for God.*

All theology appears reprehensible and, therefore, subject to temptation by God, firstly, to the extent that even if it should all the time not lose sight of the first commandment, it scarcely seems able to avoid weighty transgressions of the second and third commands concerning worship of images and the taking of God's name in vain. "When words are many, transgression is not lacking" (Proverbs 10:19). Where and when was theology ever untainted by the enormous presumption of treating its positive and negative as well as its critical concepts, along with its linguistic forms and constructions, as identifications of reality instead of as parables? Theoretically, of course, it zealously denies this attempt, but practically it undertakes it all the same. When has theology not attempted to entrap the divine Logos in its analogies, setting these analogies, in fact, on the throne of God, worshiping and proclaiming them or recommending and acclaiming them for worship and proclamation? And where or when was it ever free from the frivolity of treating its indications of God's work and word in a smooth flow of thoughts and speech, just as though they were roulette chips, which can be tossed on the table of general conversation according to whim or desire, in hopes of winning hard cash? How could God be present there, or present other than in silence, even though something fine might well be said about him? Such inversions necessarily bring to light the whole disproportion between God and that which man in confrontation with him believes he can permit himself. Since God cannot condone this disproportion, he cannot be for or with the theologians and their theology, but only against them.

The work of theology, secondly, appears subject to judgment, to the extent that the development of all kinds of human *vanity* seems almost necessarily to belong to its very procedure. At the very point where everyone should simply try and do his best; where he should look neither to the right nor to the left; and where even his finest and most costly elaborations should make him deeply troubled and sincerely humbled—at this point the question, "Who is the greatest among us?" seems to be at least as interesting as the plain and modest question about the matter at hand. Yes, who is the greatest? Who exercises the strongest attraction and has, for instance, the most people in his church? Who has the most children for confirmation? Or who, in the university, attracts the largest audiences?—a question which here and there can even lead one to probe the collective vanity of whole theological faculties! Whose books receive the most attention and are perhaps even read? Who is called on for lectures both at home and abroad? In short, who conducts his business in the most resplendent fashion? It might be thought that the statement, "See how they love one another!" (if such a thing could be said of any group of men), might apply pre-eminently to theologians. But, in fact, they themselves are nearly proverbial for their zealousness about all that they continually have in their hearts and on their lips to say against one another, and for what they put in black and white against one another with deep mistrust and a massive air of superiority. This was done more coarsely in days of old; today, as a rule, it happens softly, politely, but all the more pointedly. Melanchthon certainly was not alone when he thought he should expressly add, in the list of clarifications and improve-

ments which he expected in the hereafter, liberation
from the *rabies theologorum,* the fury of the theologians.
No doubt there will always be serious enough reason for
this *rabies,* and even the eagerness to do the job best
and be the greatest could, at least from afar, have something to do with the justified concern about the domi-
nance of truth in the Church, a concern demanded of
the theologian in eminent fashion. But where and when
was there not a continual trespassing of the boundary
between this concern and the sphere of a conceitedness
and obstinacy which are but disgustingly human? And
how should God be present in this sphere other than in
wrath and, as a result, in silence? What else could the
theology of these theologians be—when they contend for
themselves and against one another (regardless of how
good they might otherwise be)—than theology that is
placed in temptation by its own object?

Theology is, thirdly, reprehensible and open to temptation to the extent that it is, by its very nature, a *theo-
retical* work. In theology a man is no doubt bent over
the Scriptures, harkening to the voice of the great
teachers of all centuries, and devoted to the true God
and true man with, as is to be hoped, earnest piety and
the utmost exertion of his own intelligence. But in this
work he all too easily loses sight of the concrete relationship between true God and true man; he substitutes,
instead, his own reflections, meditations, and perorations,
which are based upon thought that is not controlled by
God. Theological existence, as such, always has something of the monastic life about it, including both the
peaceful intensity of monasticism, as well as its carefree
attitude and spiritual comfortableness. Is there not also
an astonishing disparity between what is important, discussed and, more or less victoriously put in action in
theology, and the errors and confusions, the sea of suffering and misery prevailing in the world that surrounds

theology? What has happened in the past, and what happens in our very own time? *There,* amidst the world, is the still "unconquered past" of the madness of dictators, the intrigues of their cliques and of the peoples who form their following; there is also the past of the stupidity of their opponents and conquerors. There are the murderers and the murdered of the concentration camps. There are Hiroshima, Korea, Algeria, and the Congo. There is the undernourishment of the greater part of mankind. There is the cold war and the sinister threat of a "hot" one, which might very well be the last. In other words, there is the stubbornly promoted end of all life on our planet. *Here,* however, in the realm of theology, is a little de-mythologizing in Marburg and a little *Church Dogmatics* in Basel. *Here* are the rediscovery of the "historical" Jesus and the glorious new discovery of a "God above God." *Here* are the discussions on baptism and eucharist, Law and Gospel, Kerygma and myth, Romans 13 and the heritage of Dietrich Bonhoeffer. *Here* are ecumenical discussions and Church councils. Nothing of all this should be underestimated, much less disparaged; doubtless the perspiration of many noble souls has not been poured out in vain over all these enterprises.

But Kyrie Eleison!—what is the real relationship to everything that simultaneously happened *there?* Could not theology be a luxury occupation, and could not we all be in the process of fleeing from the living God? Could not such a questionable theologian as Albert Schweitzer have chosen the better part (precisely from the point of view of the object of theology), and along with him the first and best of those who here and there have attempted, without any theological reflection, to heal the wounded, to feed the hungry, to give drink to the thirsty, and to prepare a home for the orphaned? Is not all theology distinguished by the fact that in the shadow of the great need of the world (and also of the Church in the world), it seems to have so much time and so little haste? Even if it does not deny the Second Coming of Jesus Christ, it is apparently occupied with other matters and looks toward its redemption in this coming with a remarkably easygoing air. I draw no conclusions—none, for instance, such as those suggested by a young man from Germany (obviously somewhat delirious) who recently proposed to me in a friendly manner during a visit that I should burn all my books—together with those of Bultmann, Ernst Fuchs, and a few others—as wholly worthless. I am only asking *questions*. But they are urgent questions which, by the very fact that they arise and cannot simply be brushed aside, represent a form of the wrath of God by which all that we produce as theology is assailed.

Fourthly, however, theology appears reprehensible and open to temptation by God with respect to its own achievements. How often has it actually led the Church and aided her service in the world, as it should have done? How often has it not, on the contrary, misled the Church and hindered her service? Either it did not itself abide in the school of the Scriptures, desiring, instead, to bar its entrance to others as well, or, without noticing it, it howled with the wolves of the current day, or it reacted headstrongly and arbitrarily against the present, driving out one wolf only to throw the gate open to others. Is it not dismaying to see how even the greatest and most famous theologians, even an Athanasius, Augustine, Thomas Aquinas, Luther, Zwingli, or Calvin, not to speak of Kierkegaard or Kohlbrügge, have left really catastrophic traces behind, in spite of their positive influence and results? When was theology ever safe from reading alien or even contradictory things into Scriptures at the same time that it undertook to explain them? When it recognizes one thing properly, it misreads something else all the more thoroughly. At one point it bears witness, while at another point it denies all the more sharply. Here it throws a spotlight on the truth, but there it solemnly and determinedly puts the truth under a bushel. In which of its forms would theology not be required to apply first of all to itself the "Woe to you!" spoken by Jesus to the scribes, instead of applying this, as theology so loves to do, to its contemporary opponents? But if theology stands under that "Woe to you!" it stands in temptation. It stands judged by the question as to whether it might not be working in the service of the Antichrist instead of in the service of Jesus Christ.

Let us pause a moment. Things would not be so bad if this last and most potent threat to theology only involved certain crises which, although more or less acute, were temporary and pertained only to one or another special theology. No doubt this threat actually erupts in acute crises, in recognizable accidents in the history of theology, and at special times and places. But potentially, theology stands under this threat at *every* time and place. There is no theology which could live otherwise than by the mercy of God. No theology, therefore, can be proper and useful other than by the experience of God's judgment.

And from another viewpoint, things would also not be so bad if all that was involved was the temptation of theology by the devil. To a large measure, if not altogether, the devil may be the explanation of the menace confronting theology, where its solitude and doubt are concerned. Following a famous example, the theologian may occasionally throw an ink well at the devil, and when all else fails he should do this courageously. But with respect to temptation, such an action would not be an appropriate measure, since temptation is an action of *God*. It is an element of the grace of God, which is granted even to the theologian and his curious work. In its complete and terrible harshness (as the consuming fire of God's love, we said previously), temptation must serve for the salvation of theology and its radical purification. Obviously there cannot and may not be any wish to flee from temptation. It obviously demands being endured and borne. Whenever it is not endured and borne, theology cannot be a happy science.

"Endure and bear!" was our advice (or, more precisely, our watchword) with respect to the endangering of theology by solitude, doubt, and temptation. Let no one expect that this advice will be surpassed and supplanted at the close of this third series of our lectures by some other phrase that sounds easier and more pleasant. If this were the case, the fact would become evident that what was said previously about the threats posed for theology and the theologians should, in the final analysis, not be taken too seriously. And the still worse consequence would be that we would, by such a substitution, have turned our backs upon the very best thing that emerges from this whole shadowy complex of dangers. All that we are permitted (and required) to do is to meditate on the positive significance of this demanding endurance and bearing of solitude, doubt, and temptation. To what does our watchword, "Endure and bear," point? Indeed, if we turn ourselves toward that to which it points, we may find that it has no need at all for another and better phrase to surpass and supplant it.

"Endure and bear!" undoubtedly reminds us first of all that an inevitable and ineradicable distress must be reckoned with wherever theology is concerned. What we know as theology and, consequently, as theological existence is always assaulted by the threefold menace, and will continue to face great danger always and at every place, as long as time endures. We might well wish it were otherwise, for the threat is painful, agonizing, and, in its last and most intense form, even deadly. The spiteful remark that theology is a type of sickness is not altogether unjustified! At its ultimate and greatest extreme, theology might well be called a "sickness unto death." The end of this sickness cannot be predicted; no one can expect to be cured of it by proper treatment or by a natural process of healing. Should anyone wish things were different, he would be well advised not to get involved from the very beginning. He is no proper theologian who supposes he might be allowed, or even required and enabled, to deny or avoid the endangering of theology and the theologian, brushing it aside or putting it out of his mind because it means distress and suffering. There are plenty of other occupations which, apparently at least, are less weighty and dangerous. From beginning to end, the theological task can only be undertaken and carried out at the cost of that characteristically sharp unpleasantness which encounters the theologian through every one of the threats we have described. The theologian must endure and bear this unpleasantness.

But one thing is excluded by the very fact that the theologian endures and bears what must be endured and borne. The unpleasantness he sustains cannot induce him to give in, flee, or capitulate, to refuse to take up or continue the work of theology, or to let its problem fall by the wayside. Although endurance and submission may be performed with fatigue, sighs, and groans, or blood, sweat, and tears, they remain the opposite of all sorrowful resignation and surrender, even when circumstances become far worse than had been supposed in advance. "To bear" means to bear the burden laid upon oneself, in spite of its painfulness, instead of throwing it aside or passing it on to someone else. And "to endure," to be constant or persistent, means to resist with one's back pressed against the wall, to refuse to retreat regardless of the cost, and to stand fast under all circumstances. To endure and bear means not to be slack but to show a little courage for God's sake. If, of course, anyone was unwilling or unable to show a little courage as a theologian, he should be advised not to become involved at all. But why should he not be willing and able to show just a little courage?

Looking back on our last three lectures, let us draw this one basic and final conclusion: There can be no theology without much distress, but also none without courage in distress. This is the double meaning of "Endure and bear!"

We are not weakening our initial, as well as ultimate, thesis when we proceed to the following statement: The danger and distress of theology contain *hope*—and this hope is not somewhere alongside or behind them but within themselves. By saying this, we have not withdrawn anything from our thesis, nor have we added anything new. We have only repeated it in its full import. The danger *nevertheless* contains hope; this is nothing less than the "Nevertheless" of Psalms 73:23. And the summons and permission to take up and perform theological work are inseparable from the fact that this distress is endured and borne; hope exists not *after* this fact but *in* this very fact. Let us attempt to understand this situation somewhat better.

The work of theology is oriented in every respect to the reality of God's work and the truth of his Word. This truth—radically superior to theology—is presupposed for it in the manner of a radical *pre*supposition. At every time and place, this truth is the *future* of theology. It is not something placed in its hands or put in its charge, something at the disposal of its thought and speech, surrendered and delivered up to the control and rule of the theologian. At every time and place, theology can only look and move toward this truth. Theology is aroused and commissioned as a function in the service of the community by God's work and word

in their awesome majesty. But it is aroused and commissioned as the work of men; and, as the work of men,
it is obviously and necessarily called in question and
endangered. Those involved in this work find themselves
isolated, plagued by doubt, and ultimately tempted,
humbled, accused, and condemned (along with their
work) by that majestic reality and truth upon which
their gaze is fixed. How could it be otherwise? Human
work and words cannot stand before the divine work
and word; in relation to these, the former can only fall
and crumble.

The judgment which encounters theology is what we
have considered in our previous three lectures. Were
theology to receive any special honor—an honor which
might exceed that of other human acts or human science
—it could consist only in the dangerous assaults which
menace it in such a striking and unmistakable way.
Anyone who wishes, may point his finger at this sickness
suffered by theology; the theologian is the last who
could overlook or deny the fact that such illness befalls
him. This is the payment theology must make for the
extraordinary ambition of its enterprise in devoting
itself to this object, in posing and answering the question about truth with respect to this reality and truth.

Theology, therefore, has no right to complain about
the fact that such threats befall it. By what right could
it ever withdraw from this endangering? Things cannot be otherwise if (as should be the case) theology is
dedicated to the superior work and word of God. It is
and remains informed about all that threatens it; it
must always reconsider it; and it must proclaim abroad
the definite fact that *all* flesh is accused, condemned, and
radically assailed by such encounter. All flesh is en-
compassed here—the moral as well as the immoral, the
pious as well as the impious, all human thought, will,
and action, the most excellent as well as the less ex-

cellent. There is no human work or word which can avoid becoming dust and ashes in the fire that proceeds from that source. How could theology delude itself and claim that its own work and word would form an exception? To the extent that it fancied and claimed such an exception for itself, it would again turn its back on the work and word of God. It would forfeit its object and become an empty train of thought or a play on words. And to the same extent, theology would also isolate itself, divorcing itself from the community and world, in whose midst it must perform its service.

Theology can be useful only when it does not retreat from the divine judgment that accompanies the work of all men, but, instead, unreservedly exposes and submits itself to this judgment. Only by not rejecting or resisting the threat that encounters it, but, instead, acknowledging its propriety, reconciling itself to it, and enduring and bearing it, can theology become useful. When theology does *this*, it shows by its own behavior the reality and truth of its encounter with God's work and word, with the object that gives it its foundation as a science. And when theology does *this*, it confirms the fact that it has a legitimate place and service in the midst of the community and mankind surrounding it. When theology confesses its own solidarity with all flesh and with the whole world under God's judgment, it receives *hope* in the grace of God which is the mystery of this judgment. This hope is a present reality in which theology may also participate and do its own work.

It is not enough to observe that there is no ground for complaint about the fact that theology must suffer *as much as* all men's thoughts, intentions, and performances in other realms are exposed to suffering. But it must be stated that theology must suffer even *more* than those. God's painful opposition to men's work, an opposition which includes both his gracious encourage-

ment and the hope he grants to men and to the whole
world, must necessarily appear more clearly and harshly
(not to say more spectacularly) in relation to the theologian than to other men. God more clearly opposes the
theologian, who is *ex professo* concerned with the communion between God and man and between man and
God, than he opposes the work of the doctor, engineer, or
artist, of the farmer, craftsman, or worker, of the sales-
man or clerk. How much of the yawning abyss which
runs through all human existence can, in these professions, remain relatively and provisionally concealed by
the substantial quality, boldness, and tangible success of
human intentions and achievements! It is quite fitting
that what the theologian undertakes and accomplishes
must dispense with such concealment. Were this not the
case, he or his environment would be deluding itself!
With every step that the theologian ventures, he has
occasion to comprehend once more and unambiguously
the fragmentary character of *his* questions and answers,
his research and speech, *his* discoveries and formulations. There is no thought that he thinks and no sentence that he speaks which do not remind him, as well
as others, that God is no doubt good, but that man, even
in his best endeavors and deeds, is not good at all. What
exegesis, sermon, or theological treatise is worthy of
being called "good"? And is it not obviously sheer nonsense to speak of "famous" theologians or even theological "geniuses," not to mention considering oneself as
such? Paul Gerhardt is right: "The Lord alone is king,
but I am a faded flower."* Who else would have so
much and so direct occasion and reason for applying this
verse to himself and his productions as has the theologian? This is a strange advantage that seems to be due
him in comparison with other men! Let him never be
ashamed of it! Otherwise he would be ashamed of the

* From Paul Gerhardt's hymn, *"Du Meine Seele, singe,"* 1653.

Gospel, which is entrusted to him in such a special way. He would be ashamed of the special object of his science, and also of the special service which has been made his, and finally of the special hope in which he is allowed to carry out his service.

The mystery of the special threat to theology is precisely its special hope. Precisely for the sake of this hope, the theologian is made to suffer from solitude, doubt, and temptation more noticeably than other men. By the very fact that he grasps this hope, not somewhere alongside, but in the very center of his special exposure to danger, he may, should, and can endure and bear the danger that confronts him. With Abraham (Romans 4:18), he believes in hope, where there is nothing to be hoped for (*contra spem in spem*). Does he not know, has he not heard, and is not this his own most personal theme: that God in his Son came into the world to heal those who are sick and to seek and save those who are lost? What if his cause or even he himself (to the extent that he is devoted to this cause) should seem quite exceptionally sick and lost? Why should he not conclude from this, when he takes up this cause and endures and bears what must be suffered for its sake, that he is allowed to be a man who is sought, healed, and saved by God in quite a special way?

At this point we may and must take a further step and attempt to understand somewhat more concretely the relationship between the radical endangering of theology and its hope.

In God's judgment all theological as well as human existence can have no justification, no fame, no endurance. It can only turn to dust and ashes before God. Yet just this God is the hope of man's work and word, because God's wrath is the fire of his love, and because his grace is hidden and effective under the contradiction (*contrarium*) of his judgment, and draws near to its revelation in this judgment upon all theological as well as human existence. This very God is the promise and stimulus, according to which theology may and must be risked in its entirely endangered situation. God is this hope precisely at the point where human works and words are manifestly nothing better than demonstrations of their precariousness and powerlessness. God may, can, and should be man's hope precisely and preeminently in this hopeless situation, *contra spem in spem*. This is the very situation in which, at God's command, one should cast one's net. When understood in this sense, God's radical endangering of all human and, especially, all theological existence is only a relative and not an absolute endangering. It is one which can be endured and borne.

The God of whom we speak is no god imagined or devised by men. The grace of the gods who are imagined or devised by men is usually a conditional grace, to be merited and won by men through supposedly good works, and not the true grace which gives itself freely. Instead of being hidden under the form of a contradiction, *sub contrario*, and directed to man through radical endangering and judgment, man's imagined grace is usually directly offered and accessible in some way to him and can be rather conveniently, cheaply, and easily appropriated. Evangelical theology, on the other hand, is to be pursued in hope, though as a human work it is radically questioned by God, found guilty in God's judgment and verdict—and though collapsing long before it reaches its goal, it relies on God who himself seeks out, heals, and saves man and his work. This God is the hope of theology.

What we have just said about evangelical theology cannot be said about any of the theologies that are devoted to the gods of man's devising. From beginning to end we have here spoken of the God of the Gospel. He is the object of theology, which is threatened in so many ways. He, who is its object, is also the one who menaces it. But when he does this, he is also the hope of theology. He puts it to shame, even to the uttermost extremes of shame. But he is its hope, he will vindicate the hope placed in him. He himself will protect theology, more than any other human work, from falling into utter disgrace.

We say this simply in view of the fact that the God of the Gospel is the God who has acted and revealed himself in Jesus Christ. Jesus Christ is God's work and word. He is the fire of God's love, by which all theological existence is consumed even more radically than all human existence. He is the Judge before whom all men can only fall and perish along with their knowledge and deeds—and this is known best by those who know Him best. *Ecce homo!* Behold the man! It was in *his* person that Adam (and first and foremost the pious, learned, and wise Adam) was stamped as a transgressor, displayed in his nakedness, condemned, scourged, crucified, and killed. At the conclusion of this judgment, the storm of radical danger and judgment broke overwhelmingly upon *him* more than upon anyone before or after him, together with the distress of solitude, doubt, and temptation. He and he alone is the object of evangelical theology.

If it is true that God in Jesus Christ is the object of theology, how could theological work be done other than in the shadow of the judgment passed upon man on the cross at Golgotha? If theology signifies and is the knowledge of God in *him*, for what else could it be determined other than to display the signs and tokens of the threat which first and foremost encountered and became transparent through *him?* Theological work suffers this danger in solidarity with the work of the community, as well as with all human work; yet it suffers it in a special way. Kierkegaard once mockingly asked, "What is a professor of theology?" and replied just as mockingly, "He is a professor because someone else was crucified." That is indeed what the theologian must now pay for. If he tried to evade that or to escape the distress of his solitude, doubt, and temptation, what more would he have to do with Jesus Christ? To know God in Jesus Christ obviously has to include obeying the God who acts and reveals himself in Christ and who reconciles the world with himself in *Him*. This knowledge means following after Christ. Why should theology, as *theologia crucis,* not be willing to take up its own cross and suffering, which, in relation to Christ's, are quite modest? Why should it not endure and bear, without grumbling and rebellion, whatever must be suffered in communion with him?

But this is not all. Hidden deep beneath this inescapable No is God's Yes as the meaning of his work and word. This Yes is the reconciliation of the world with God, the fulfillment of his covenant with men, which he has accomplished and revealed in Jesus Christ. Jesus Christ has carried out the judgment of all men, of their existence and actions. For he, the appointed judge of all men, delivered himself up for a unique ministry. He stepped into the place of those who were to be judged, and permitted himself to be judged for them and their liberation. The secret of the judgment carried out on Golgotha is actually not God's rejection but his grace, not men's destruction but their salvation. It is the new creation of a free man who lives in faithfulness that corresponds to God's faithfulness, in peace with God and as a witness to his glory. The God who acts and reveals himself in the death of his dear Son forms, no doubt, a real and deathly peril, but he is also the vivifying hope of theological, as well as human and Christian, existence.

Though it is hard to believe, it is true that Jesus Christ has, indeed, died for the theologians also, rising again from the dead in order to reveal this fact and to give substance to their hope. The theologians will have to abide by the fact that the living Jesus Christ, who is the foundation and object of their quest, who makes theology possible and rules and sustains it, is none other than he who was crucified. *Ave crux unica spes mea!*— Hail, O Cross, my *sole* hope! When theology holds fast to this fact, it can, may, and will be also a *theologia gloriae*, a theology of glory in faithfulness to its character as *theologia crucis*. It may be a theology of hope in the glory of the children of God, a glory that is already revealed in the resurrection of Jesus Christ and is to be revealed anew, at the very last, for the benefit of all creatures and, therefore, also for theology and its work. Gazing toward him who is the hope of imperiled theology, the theologians are permitted, along with all other men, to lift up their heads. "If we have died with Christ, we believe [we trust] that we shall also live with him" (Rom. 6:8). Since their death is not separated from, but in communion with, him, their life is also not separated from, but in communion with, him. They build on a firm foundation if they work in profound happiness as well as in profound terror. Since they are his followers, they are with him, but as well they are also deeply humbled and deeply comforted by him. The theologian will then act not only with "a bit of bravery" concerning the solitude, doubt, and temptation that he must still endure so long as his hope in the Lord remains hidden by the exposure of his work to great danger; he will also know how to endure and bear all this in *alacritas, hilaritas,* and even *laetitia spiritualis* (to speak with Calvin), in alacrity, hilarity, and spiritual joy, in the joyousness of the Holy Spirit. He will endure all this as the No which is nevertheless only the husk of the Yes, a Yes which is valid even for him at this very time and place and which, at the last, will break through with irresistible power.

IV THEOLOGICAL WORK

Theological *work* is the leading theme of the fourth and final series of these lectures. In the first series we discussed the special *place* that is assigned theology by its object; in the second series, the manner of existence of the *theologian;* and in the third series, the *danger* to which theology and the theologian are exposed. In the remaining four lectures our attention will be occupied by what must be done, performed, and accomplished in theology.

At the outset, two things must be obvious after all that has immediately preceded this lecture. *First,* all theological work can be undertaken and accomplished only amid great distress, which assails it on all sides. But though this distress may befall theology from within and without, it is ultimately caused by the object of theology itself. Without judgment and death there is no grace and no life for anybody or anything, and, least of all, for theology. For this reason there is no courage in theology without humility, no exaltation without abasement, no courageous deeds without the knowledge that by our power alone nothing at all can be done. But *secondly,* theological work should be boldly begun and carried forward because, hidden in the great distress in which alone it can take place, its still greater hope and impulse are present. Precisely in judgment is grace displayed and granted; precisely in death is life awakened and sustained. Precisely in humility may courage be taken. In theology, precisely he who abases himself is he who may, indeed must, rise up. Precisely the knowledge that by our own power nothing at all can be accomplished, allows and requires courageous action. Wherever theology becomes and remains faithful to its object, both God's grace and God's judgment, and consequently both the sinner's death and his salvation, must be taken equally seriously. In spite of all solitude and doubt, theology will be faithful to its object only and precisely when it allows itself to be tempted by it. While theological work is in great danger arising from judgment and sin, it is yet to be undertaken with still greater hope in grace and salvation. While in the following we shall certainly continue keeping the first in sight, what concerns us in the last lectures is specifically the second member of these contrasting pairs.

The first and basic act of theological work is *prayer*. Prayer must, therefore, be the keynote of all that remains to be discussed. Undoubtedly, from the very beginning and without intermission, theological work is also *study*; in every respect it is also *service;* and finally it would certainly be in vain were it not also an act of love. But theological work does not merely begin with prayer and is not merely accompanied by it; in its totality it is peculiar and characteristic of theology that it can be performed only in the act of prayer. In view of the danger to which theology is exposed and to the hope that is enclosed within its work, it is natural that without prayer there can be no theological work. We should keep in mind the fact that prayer, as such, is work; in fact, very hard work, although in its execution the hands are most fittingly not moved but folded. Where theology is concerned, the rule *Ora et labora!* is valid under all circumstances—pray and work! And the gist of this rule is not merely that *orare*, although it should be the beginning, would afterward be only incidental to the execution of the *laborare*. The rule means, moreover, that the *laborare* itself, and as such, is essentially an *orare*. Work must be that sort of act that has the manner and meaning of a prayer in all its dimensions, relationships, and movements.

Some of the most significant dimensions of the unity of prayer and theological work are the following:

1. Proper and useful theological work is distinguished by the fact that it takes place in a realm which not only has open windows (which in themselves are admittedly good and necessary) facing the surrounding life of the Church and world, but also and above all has a skylight. That is to say, theological work is opened *by* heaven and God's work and word, but it is also open *toward* heaven and God's work and word. It cannot possibly be taken for granted that this work is performed in this *open* realm, open toward the object of theology, its source and goal, and in this way open toward its great menace and the still greater hope which is founded upon its object. If theological work should attempt to hide itself from danger and hope, it would soon find itself locked in a closed, barred, stuffy, and unlit room. In itself, the realm of theology is no larger and better than the realm of human questions and answers, human inquiry, thought, and speech. What theologian is there who is not continually surprised to find, even when he endeavors wholly and perhaps very seriously to press forward to relatively true and important insights and statements, that he is moving about in a human, all too human, circle like a squirrel in a cage? He may be listening more and more attentively to the witness of the Bible, and understanding more and more lucidly the confessions of faith, the voices of the Church fathers and of contemporaries, all the time combining these with the required openness to the world. As he lingers here and there on different occasions, he may, no doubt, come upon problems that are certainly interesting, or perceptions that are thought provoking or even exciting. The only flaw is that the whole subject (and, as a result, each particular topic as well) does not begin to shed light or to take on contours and constant features. In that case it makes no

difference whether the theologian is totally devoted to his cause or whether the windows are opened as wide as possible on all sides; his whole subject, nevertheless, refuses to display its unity, necessity, helpfulness, and beauty.

What, then, is lacking? The flaw is that however industriously he labors at his work or however widely and broadly it may be extended, the theologian exists basically alone in all his work. His work takes place in an area that unfortunately is vertically sealed off; it neither receives nor beholds light from above. It opens no skylight toward heaven. What can and must happen to remedy this predicament?

A special measure must obviously be taken; the circular movement must be interrupted; a Sabbath day must be inserted and celebrated. The purpose of the Sabbath is not to eliminate the working days or to divest them of their proper tasks, but rather to obtain for them precisely the light from above which they lack. How can this happen? What can and should happen is that the theologian for a moment should turn away from all his efforts in the performance of the *intellectus fidei*. At such a moment he can and should turn exclusively toward the object of theology, himself, to God. But what else is such a turning to God than the turning of prayer? For in prayer a man temporarily turns away from his own efforts. This move is necessary precisely for the sake of the duration and continuation of his own work. Every prayer has its beginning when a man puts himself (together with his best and most accomplished work) out of the picture. He leaves himself and his work behind in order once again to recollect that he stands before God. How could he ever find it unnecessary to recollect this fact continually and anew? He stands before the God who, in his work and word, is man's Lord, Judge, and Saviour. He recognizes also that this God stands before him, or rather draws near to him, in His work and word. This is the mighty, holy, and merciful God who is the great threat and the still greater hope of man's work.

Prayer begins with the movement in which a man wishes and seeks to win new clarity about the fact that "God is the one who rules." A man prays, not in order to sacrifice his work or even to neglect it, but in order that it may not remain or become unfruitful work, so that he may do it under the illumination and, consequently, under the rule and blessing of God. As much as any other work, theological work is encouraged and directed to begin with this conscious movement of prayer. He who wants to do this responsibly and hopefully must know clearly who the one is who is both the threat and the hope of theology. Specifically, the question and inquiry about God will always demand and form a special activity. Other activities must retreat behind this one for a while (just as the activities of the week retreat behind the activity of the Sabbath). They do this just in order to be proper activities in their own right. They are disclosed and set in the proper light by prayer.

2. The object of theological work is not some *thing* but some *one*. He is not a highest or absolute something (even if this were "the ground of Being," or the like). This object is not an "It" but a "He." And He, this One, exists not as an idle and mute being for Himself, but precisely in His *work* which is also His *Word*.

The task of theological work consists in listening to Him, this One who speaks through His work, and in rendering account of His Word to oneself, the Church, and the world. Primarily and decisively, however, theological work must recognize and demonstrate that the Word of this One is no neutral announcement, but rather the critical moment of history and the communion between God and man. This Word is God's *address* to men. *"I* am the Lord your God, who led *you* out of the land of Egypt, out of the house of bondage. *You* shall have no other gods before *me."* Only as such an address can this Word be spoken and heard, and only as such is it the Word of the truth of God's work, the truth of God himself. For this reason all human thought and speech in relation to God can have only the character of a *response* to be made to God's Word.

Human thought and speech cannot be *about* God, but must be directed *toward* God, called into action by the divine thought and speech directed to men, and following and corresponding to this work of God. Human thought and speech would certainly be false if they bound themselves to a divine "It" or "something," since God is a person and not a thing. But human thought and speech concerning God could also be false and would at any rate be unreal if they related themselves to him in the *third* person. What is essential for human language is to speak of men in the first person and of God in the *second* person. True and proper language concerning God will always be a response to God, which overtly or covertly, explicitly or implicitly, thinks and speaks of God exclusively in the second person. And this means that theological work must really and truly take place in the form of a liturgical act, as invocation of God, and as prayer.

There remains a veil of theological thought and speech in the third person, but this veil always affords a glimpse beyond itself. In a direct unveiling of this situation, Anselm of Canterbury surpassed the first form of his doctrine of God (which was called and was a "Monologion") by a second form, which he called a "Proslogion"! In this second work he actually unfolded all that he had to say concerning God's existence and essence in the form of direct address to God, as a single prayer from beginning to end. And at the beginning of the eighteenth century, obviously in recollection of the same fact, the Lutheran David Hollaz made at least the conclusion of every single article of his dogmatics a *Suspirium,* a sigh of explicit prayer. Any theology which would not even consider the necessity to respond to God personally could only be false theology. It would exchange what is real for what is unreal if it did not unfailingly keep sight of this I-Thou relationship in which God is man's God and man is God's man. Implicitly and explicitly, proper theology will have to be a *Proslogion, Suspirium,* or prayer. It will meditate on the fact that God can be its object only because he is the acting and speaking subject upon whom all depends. Every liturgical movement in the Church arrives too late if its theology is not itself a liturgical movement from the very beginning, if it is not set in motion by *Proskynesis,* i.e., by adoration.

3. Theological work is distinguished from other kinds of work by the fact that anyone who desires to do this work cannot proceed by building with complete confidence on the foundation of questions that are already settled, results that are already achieved, or conclusions that are already arrived at. He cannot continue to build today in any way on foundations that were laid yesterday by himself, and he cannot live today in any way on the interest from a capital amassed yesterday. His only possible procedure every day, in fact every hour, is to begin anew at the beginning. And in this respect theological work can be exemplary for all intellectual work. Yesterday's memories can be comforting and encouraging for such work only if they are identical with the recollection that this work, even yesterday, had to begin at the beginning and, it is to be hoped, actually began there. In theological science, continuation always means "beginning once again at the beginning." In

view of the radical exposure of this science to danger, this is obviously the only possible way. The endangering of theology is strong enough to cut the ground away from under the feet of the theologian time and again and to compel him to look around anew for ground on which he can stand as if he had never stood on such ground before. And above all, the ever-new start is the only possible way because the object of theology is the living God himself in his free grace, Israel's protector who neither slumbers nor sleeps. It makes no difference whether theological work is done with attention to the witness of Scriptures, with the reassuring connection to the *communio sanctorum* of all times, and certainly also with a thankful memory of the knowledge previously attained by theology. If God's goodness is new every morning, it is also every morning a fully undeserved goodness which must give rise to new gratitude and renewed desire for it.

For this reason every act of theological work must have the character of an offering in which everything is placed before the living God. This work will be such an offering in all its dimensions, even if it involves the tiniest problem of exegesis or dogmatics, or the clarification of the most modest fragment of the history of the Church of Jesus Christ, but, above all, if it is the preparation of a sermon, lesson, or Bible study. In this act of offering, every goal that previously was pursued, every knowledge that previously had been won, and, above all, every method that was previously practiced and has supposedly proved its worth, must be thrown into the cauldron once again, delivered up to the living God, and proffered to him as a total sacrifice.

Theological work cannot be done on any level or in any respect other than by freely granting the free God room to dispose at will over everything that men may already have known, produced, and achieved, and over

all the religious, moral, intellectual, spiritual, or divine
equipage with which men have traveled. In the present
continuation of what was won yesterday, the continuity
between yesterday and today and between today and
tomorrow must be submitted to God's care, judgment,
and disposing. Theology can only be a really free and
happy science in a continually new performance of this
voluntary offering. If it does not want to succumb to
hardening of the arteries, barrenness, and stubborn fatigue, its work should at no step of the way become a
routine or be done as if it were the action of an autom-
aton. Because it has to be ever renewed, ever original,
ever ready to be judged by God himself and by God
alone, theology must be an act of prayer. The work of
theology is done when nothing else is accomplished but
the humble confession, "Not as I will, but as thou wil-
lest!"

This prayer and confession will not harm the readiness and willingness with which a man accepts the task
of a theologian, in performing the requirements of the
intellectus fidei, to seek the truth, to inquire and think
about it, to crack the hard nuts, and to split the thick
logs of the problems facing him. The purpose of the
ever-new subjection of theology and of the theologian to
God's will and judgment is simply this: the *intellectus
fidei* should be, remain, and ever again become a human
work that is vigorous, fresh, interesting, and helpful.
It is a fact that this work can be and is done with vigor
only when it is done not in some sort of rearmament
over against its object but in the undaunted disarma-
ment and capitulation to its object—that is to say, in
the work of prayer.

4. We now approach what is, in practical terms, the
most tangible and also, objectively, the decisive point.
Theological work is done in the form of human ques-

tions and answers. It is a seeking and finding with respect to the work and word of God.

Two problems unmistakably arise here with respect to the possibility of accomplishing this work. One stems from the side of the "subjective," the other from that of the "objective." Both are related and bound to one another. Both are problems of the living communion between God and man and man and God, and for this reason they can be solved pragmatically, never ideally, only in the history of this communion.

On the one hand (subjectively) there is the problem of the appropriateness and capability of human acts. Is this matter really taken up by a man with the purity of heart, serious intentions, clear head, and good conscience which are appropriate to it and which alone give this whole undertaking promise? In what situation, and for what theologian, could this question be positively answered other than by saying: God's grace is powerful enough to give even a man's impure heart, hesitant will, weak head, and bad conscience the capacity to ask and answer meaningfully with respect to God and his work and word. But is this grace shown to this man? And on the other hand (objectively) there is the problem of the presence of God in his self-disclosure, without which even the most earnest questions and answers with respect to him would necessarily be void of an object, and therefore in vain. Once again, this problem can be positively answered only by saying: God's grace is free and powerful enough for this work too. God will do it himself. But will grace really *occur* in this sense? In this, as in the former case, grace would obviously not be grace if there was any reason to assume that grace—God making man receptive for him and himself for man—will automatically or necessarily occur. If *grace* is what occurs there, God can only be appealed to for it, entreated for it, and called upon for

its demonstration. Only when theological work begins
with this entreaty can it be risked in view of these two
problems. Only when it is upheld by this supplication and
repeatedly returns to it can theological work be done with
prospects of possible fulfillment. What God will be asked
for is the *wondrous* thing, that man's blind eyes and deaf
ears may be opened, that he may be permitted to do and
to hear God's work and word. And, at the same time,
something still more wonderful will be sought by
prayer: that God's work and word may not be withdrawn, but may, instead, be disclosed to the eyes and ears
of this man. Gazing upon himself, Anselm prayed:
Revela me de me ad te! Da mihi, ut intelligam!
(Reveal me from myself to thee! Grant that I may
understand!) And gazing upon God: *Redde te mihi! Da
te ipsum mihi, Deus meus!* (Restore thyself to me!
Give thyself to me, my God!) In the performance of
theological work the realization of this double act of
God (together with this double entreaty) is necessary
throughout, since God's act in both respects can occur
only as his free act of grace and wondrousness.

Properly understood, this act is still only a single
one, the very one which we called to mind at the end of
our fifth lecture: *Veni, Creator Spiritus!* In his movements from below to above and from above to below, the
one Holy Spirit achieves the opening of God for man
and the opening of man for God. Theological work,
therefore, lives by and in the petition for his coming.
All its questions, inquiries, reflections, and declarations
can only be forms of this petition. And only in God's
hearing of this entreaty is theological work at any time
a successful and useful work. Only so can it, in its total
endangering and its total dependence on God's free
grace, serve to the glory of God and the salvation of
men. God hears *genuine* prayer! And the criterion of the
genuineness of *this* prayer is that it will be made in

certainty that it will be heard. If this petition were born
of skepticism, how should the speaker really know what
he is doing when he entreats the Father in the name of
the Son for the Holy Spirit? The certainty that this
petition will be heard is consequently also the certainty
in which theological work may and should be courageously started and performed.

In prayer, theological work is the inner, spiritual, and vertically directed motion of man; while in study, although similarly external, it runs in a horizontal direction. It is also an intellectual, psychical, and physical, if not fleshly, movement. Theological work can be done only in the indissoluble unity of prayer and study. Prayer without study would be empty. Study without prayer would be blind. We are obliged now, since our consideration of prayer is completed, to attempt an interpretation of study.

In the sense that interests us, "study" is an undertaking to be pursued earnestly, zealously, and industriously; it is, in fact, a definite intellectual task objectively set for the theologian and other men. Study demands human participation, vigorously pressed forward because of man's impulse, free inclination, and desire to complete the given task. These qualifications determine who and what is or is not a *studiosus* and, in particular, a *studiosus theologiae*, a student of theology.

A definite intellectual task is set for the theologian and others by the Gospel, by the work and word of God which are attested to in the Holy Scriptures and proclaimed in the *communia sanctorum* of every day and age. If this task were not set for him, or if he should mistake and exchange it for another task (such as that of the philosopher, historian, or psychologist), he might still be a *studiosus*, but he would no longer be a *studiosus theologiae*. He would also cease to be a student of theology were he not devoted to his task with the characteristic impetus and impulse already described. A lazy student, even as a theologian, is no student at all!

It is well to clarify and expose two other self-evident matters which should be taken for granted.

First of all, theological study and the impulse which compels it are not passing stages of life. The forms which this study assumes may and must change slightly with the times. But the theologian, if he was in fact a *studiosus theologiae*, remains so even to his death. (Schleiermacher, it is reported, even in his old age, pre-fixed his signature at times with the usual German designation *"stud. theol."*)

Secondly, no one should study merely in order to pass an examination, to become a pastor, or in order to gain an academic degree. When properly understood, an examination is a friendly conversation of older students of theology with younger ones, concerning certain themes in which they share a common interest. The purpose of this conversation is to give younger participants an opportunity to exhibit whether and to what extent they have exerted themselves, and to what extent they appear to give promise of doing so in the future. The real value of a doctorate, even when earned with the greatest distinction, is totally dependent on the degree to which its recipient has conducted and maintained himself as a learner. Its worth depends, as well, entirely on the extent to which he further conducts and maintains himself as such. Only by his qualification as a learner can he show himself qualified to become a teacher. Whoever studies theology does so because to study it is (quite apart from any personal aims of the student) necessary, good, and beautiful in relationship to the service to which he has been called. Theology must possess him so completely that he can be concerned with it only in the manner of a *studiosus*.

Theological study is the contact (whether it be direct or literary) and meaningful union of pupils with their teachers—teachers who, for their part, were pupils of their own teachers. Such a regressive sequence continues until one reaches those teachers whose only chance and desire was to be the pupils of the immediate witnesses to the history of Jesus Christ which brought the history of Israel to its fulfillment. Theological study consists, therefore, in active participation in the work of that comprehensive community of teachers and learners which is found in the school of the immediate witnesses to the work and word of God.

The instruction which someone today receives from lectures, seminars, or books can be only a first and preliminary step. Such instruction can be merely an admission to the school where the theological student now hears and reads and in which, before him, his own teachers have listened, spoken, and written, gaining their knowledge, exchanging it with one another, transmitting and receiving it from one another. Ultimately and in its most decisive aspect, today's instruction is but an introduction to the source and norm of all theology: namely, the testimony of the Scriptures. Every predecessor of today's student has already attempted to understand and explain the Scriptures—in his own period, in his own way, and with his own limitations. To study theology means not so much to examine exhaustively the work of earlier students of theology as to become *their* fellow student. It means to become and to remain receptive, for they still speak, even though they may have died long ago. Serious study means to permit oneself to be stimulated by the views and insights they achieved and proclaimed, and to be guided— by their encouraging or frightening example—toward a perspective, thought, and speech which are responsible to God and man. But above all, theological study means to follow in their footsteps and to turn to the source from which they themselves were nourished, to the norm to which they had already, properly, and unqualifiedly subjected themselves. It means to hear the original testimony which made teachers out of pupils. It was to this norm that one's predecessors in theological study subordinated and directed themselves, so far as they were able.

In the light of the foregoing, theological study will have to be divided into two parts. We call them a primary and a secondary conversation. In the first conversation the student, whether he be young or old, will (like all students who preceded him) have to inquire *directly* into what the prophets of the Old Testament and the apostles of the New Testament have to say to the world, to the community of the present day, and to himself as a member of the community. In the secondary conversation the student must permit himself indirectly to be given the necessary directions and admonitions for the journey toward the answer which he seeks. Such secondary instructions are gained from theologians of the past, the recent past, and from his immediate antecedents—through examination of their biblical exegesis and dogmatics and their historical and practical inquiries. Even though he may be the most recent student of theology, he must follow in this path, for he is not the first, but, for the time being, the most contemporary of all students. No one, however, should ever confuse this secondary conversation with the primary one, lest he lose the forest for the trees. In such an eventuality, he would no longer be able to hear the echo of divine revelation in the Scriptures, for the sheer volume of patristic, scholastic, reformation, and, above all, modern academic voices would drown it out. On the other hand, no one should imagine himself so inspired or otherwise clever and wise that he can conduct the primary discussion by his own powers, dispensing with all secondary discussion with the fathers and brothers of the Church.

It scarcely needs to be added that theological study requires in this matter extraordinarily alert and circumspect attention. Theological study must always engage simultaneously in both the primary and secondary conversation. It must constantly distinguish both of these properly, but it must also properly combine them. Certainly an entire lifetime is not too long to gain and to apply some measure of this necessary attention and circumspection.

We shall now attempt a general survey of the different fields and areas of theological study, the so-called "departments" and "disciplines" of theological inquiry.

The first discipline to be named is obviously that of biblical exegesis. Exegesis of the Bible should not be simply identified with what we have just called the primary conversation that theology must conduct, for the hearing, understanding, and application of the biblical message is much more than an incidental presupposition of theological work. It is the fundamental task of all theological study. Reading or explaining biblical *texts* is, however, a special task. Since true understanding of the Bible is a problem continually posed anew, theology is originally and especially the science of the Old and New Testaments. The Old and New Testaments are the collections of the texts in which the community of Jesus Christ perpetually found itself summoned to hear the voice of the original testimony to God's work and word. This unique testimony is the source and norm of the community's doctrine and life. But the community must hear this voice *anew* at every moment. For the fulfillment of this task, the science of biblical theology is indispensable. All too many things can be imprecisely or even wrongly heard (or perhaps not even heard at all). The science of biblical theology must clarify, with ever renewed impartiality and care, what is actually written in the Scriptures and what is meant by all that is written.

Two presuppositions will make themselves felt in biblical exegesis.

The first presupposition of biblical theology is held in common with all historical-critical research, for the biblical texts are subject to the scrutiny of that research as much as they are to the scrutiny of the theologian. In order to read and understand the Bible, biblical theology must conscientiously employ all known and available means, all the rules and criteria that are applicable to grammar, linguistics, and style, as well as all the knowledge gathered in the comparative study of the history of the world, of culture, and of literature.

The second presupposition, although it belongs basically to the historical-critical type as well, is not yet, by any means, generally accepted by nontheological historical scientists. For this reason, its demands are respected more strictly in theological exegesis than by historical critics. However isolated from other sciences theological exegesis may become, this second presupposition is essential for its work. Theological exegesis presupposes that alongside the many texts extant in the world's literature, there may also be texts that, according to the intention of their authors and according to their actual character, require that they be read and explained as attestation and proclamation of a *divine* action and speech which have reportedly or really taken place in the midst of general history. It is presupposed that unless such texts are evaluated in faithfulness to this character, their real intention will inevitably be missed. Beyond what such texts say, in conformance to this special character, they can—so theological exegesis assumes—yield no essential information. The assumption that they call for any subsequent inquiry into facts—facts which might lie concealed behind their message or which might have been alienated from their original character and meaning by the prophets' and apostles' "interpretation," or which would have been previously independent of this interpretation and ought now to be singled out and presented according to their true nature—is by-passed. Theological exegesis presupposes that the existence of these texts makes the success of such an inquiry practically impossible. It presupposes that there are texts whose statements (if they are understood at all) can be endorsed by their readers only with unbelief, i.e., with a milder or sharper form of skepticism, or with faith. But the skeptics among those historically-critically minded have to be asked: Why should there not also be, according to their own sober historical-critical judgment, texts that are purely kerygmatic and that can be fittingly interpreted only as such? The science of biblical theology presupposes that it has to deal with such texts, particularly in the Old and New Testaments.

What these texts express can no doubt be objectively perceived, much like the content of all other texts in world literature. But to be *understood* in their own sense, the biblical texts call for either the No of unbelief or the Yes of faith. These texts can only be explained objectively by constant reference to their kerygmatic character. The science of biblical theology does not work in empty space but in the service of the community of Jesus Christ, which is founded by prophetic and apostolic testimony. It is precisely for this reason that it approaches these texts with a specific *expectation*. (Nothing more than this should be said, but also nothing less!)

Biblical theology expects that testimony to the God who calls for faith will confront it in these texts. Nevertheless, it remains unreservedly open to such questions

as: Will this expectation be fulfilled? (This is precisely
what is involved in the so-called "hermeneutical
circle.") To what extent, in what form, and through
what concrete expressions will the uniqueness which
these texts possess for the community confirm itself?
Is such exegesis "dogmatic" exegesis? An affirmative
answer has to be given only to the extent that the
science of theological exegesis rejects, at the outset,
every dogma which might forbid it the expectation just
mentioned and might declare, from the very beginning,
its vindication to be impossible. Again, is this "pneumatic" exegesis? Certainly not, in so far as such exegesis might suppose it was able to dispose over the
Scriptures on the basis of some imagined spiritual
power that it possesses. But it may be called "pneumatic" to the extent that it uses the freedom, founded
upon the Scriptures themselves, to address to them
seriously, ultimately, and definitively a strict question
about the Spirit's own testimony heard in them.

The second task of theological study is concerned, in
particular, with what we have termed the secondary
conversation. Without this secondary discussion, of
course, neither biblical exegesis nor study in any other
area of theology can be carried out. What is involved
is the study of the history of the Church, of her the-
oretical and practical life, her actions and confessions,
and thus of her theology. What is involved is the long
journey which Christian knowledge—this fundamental
element of community life—has undertaken and accomplished from the days of the prophets and apostles
until the present day. Since the history of the Church
unmistakably and continually participates in secular or
world history, and since just as unmistakably it is also a
sector of world history formed by the biblical message
from which it arises, so it must be examined in the same
manner as these. It is a history of belief, unbelief, false

belief, and superstition; a history of the proclamation
and of the denial of Jesus Christ, of deformations and
renewals of the Gospel, of obedience which Christianity
offered this Gospel or which was openly or secretly
denied it. The history of the Church, of dogmas, and of
theology is necessarily, from the perspective of this
community of saints and sinners, an object of theological study. Moreover, the community of every contemporary age is included in the ranks of this great community and must be assessed by the same criteria.

One condition for the fruitfulness of such inquiry is
that the gaze of the inquirer come to rest and remain
immovably fixed upon the *concretissimum* of the theme
of this history. Although his gaze is fixed *there,* he
maintains, nevertheless, a spirited and loving openness
to every particular of that great event, an openness that
overlooks none of its lights and none of its shadows. If
anyone is unfamiliar with this theme and fails to keep
it in view, how can he be able to understand and narrate
Church history? The *other* condition is that Gottfried
Arnold's splendid program of an "Impartial History of
the Church and of Heretics" should be carried out
more successfully. Reversing the method that was usual
up to his time, Arnold took up *only* the cause of the heretics against the Church, instead of supporting, as well,
the Church against the heretics.

The theological science of history does not desire to
pass judgment on the world. It will also not attempt, by
taking over some guiding principle from a philosophical
system (in the way that the great F. Christian Baur, in
particular, attempted it), to master the history of the
community in the time between the first and the final
coming of the Lord. It will be obliged simply to observe
and exhibit how and to what extent all that has happened and continues to happen in the history of the
community was and is flesh—flesh that is as grass or as

the flower of the field (Is. 40:6). This flesh is transitory—its essence is that it passes by and passes away. But since God is the origin and the goal of this passing history, the events of Church history are never completely bare of forgiveness and void of hope in the resurrection of the flesh. The theological science of history will calmly refrain from any total glorification of one element of the community's history or any total disqualification of another. Instead, it will weep with those who weep and rejoice with those who rejoice. It will simply let all those who lived, thought, spoke, and labored before us speak for themselves. When, for the benefit of the present community, the community's earlier life is studied and illumined in this way, the theological science of history will also serve, in a secondary and subsidiary manner, the future gathering, consolidation, and sending forth of the community.

The name that has become usual for the third principal discipline of theological study, "systematic theology," is a contradiction in terms. In the study of dogmatics and ethics, which concerns us here, there is at any rate no justification for the construction and proclamation of a system of Christian truth developed out of some definite conceptualization of it. What should rule in the community is not a concept or a principle, but solely the Word of God attested to in the Scriptures and vivified by the Holy Spirit.

What is involved in the science devoted to this Word is not merely the acknowledgment of this Word by study of Holy Scriptures and by the accompanying knowledge of the past. This Word must be *considered,* in fact *properly* considered and meditated upon. The inner relationship, the clarity, and the lucidity with which it presents itself at each particular moment will be pondered. "Proper" consideration does not mean an inclusive, conclusive, and exclusive process, as the word "systematic" could easily lead one to suppose. Proper dogmatics and ethics neither include, conclude, nor exclude; rather, like biblical exegesis and Church history, they form a science that creates openings and is itself open. At every present moment and under all circumstances, this science awaits and hopes for a future consideration of the Word of God that should be better—that is, that should be truer and more comprehensive—than all that is possible at this time. Dogmatics and ethics, moreover, cannot be proper in the sense that they might consider and interpret the Word of God according to the criteria offered either by a philosophy that is acknowledged by most people at any one time, or by certain wishes, claims, and postulates which ecclesiastical authorities might proclaim as valid. Dogmatics and ethics must function properly by considering the Word of God and by holding fast to the order, formation, architectonics, and theology prescribed at given times by this Word itself. They are proper when they make this order visible and valid for their time or for the path of knowledge pursued by the community of their time. They think freely, and they summon the community, for its part, to think and speak freely in that area of freedom granted it at given times by the Word of God. When study of so-called systematic theology has the purpose of continually recognizing this order anew, then theology may even be service for and in the community that is occupied with this task. When theology works for the attainment, maintenance, and spreading of the freedom founded on this order, then it serves the cause of appropriate action, proper renewal, and purification, as well as concentration and clarification of the statements which must be made in the community's proclamation.

Last of all, *"practical theology"* is, as the name implies, theology in transition to the practical work of the community—to proclamation. By mentioning practical theology at the end, we do not suggest that we regard it, speaking with Schleiermacher, as the "crown" of theological study nor as a merely optional appendage to the other theological disciplines. When practical theology is considered as a strictly human endeavor, we find ourselves, as in the other disciplines, on the periphery of theology's task. But when considered with respect to its object, we find ourselves, as we do in other disciplines, at the heart of the matter.

The special area of the problem of practical theology is what is today somewhat bombastically termed the "language event." Quite unsuitably, it is then customarily presented as the basic problem of exegesis and, if possible, also of dogmatics. But this event has its proper place *here,* only in practical theology. The question of practical theology is how the Word of God may be served by human words. How can this Word, which has been perceived in the testimony of the Bible and of Church history and has been considered in its contemporary self-presentation, be served also through the community for the benefit of the world that surrounds it? What is involved is not the idle question of how those who proclaim this Word should "approach" this or that modern man, or how they should "bring home" the Word of God to him. Instead, the real question is how they have to *serve* this Word by pointing to its coming. This Word has never been "brought home" to any man except *by its own freedom and power.*

The real question is the problem of the language which must be employed by those who undertake to proclaim this Word. Their speech will have to meet two conditions. In order to be an indication of *God's* Word to men, it must have the character of a *declaration.* And in order to be an indication of God's Word to *men,* it must have the character of an *address.* This *speech* can be proclamation of *this* Word only when it expresses itself quite exceptionally (as required by the source which inspires it) and at the same time quite ordinarily (to fit its purpose). It must speak in solemn *and* in commonplace tones, both sacredly and profanely. It tells *of* the history of Israel and of Jesus Christ, *and* it tells this *to* the life and action of Christians, Jews, and other contemporary men.

Theological speech is taught its content by exegesis and dogmatics, and it is given its form through the experiences of whatever psychology, sociology, or linguistics may be most trustworthy at a given moment. It is the language of Canaan and at the same time it is Egyptian or Babylonian language, or whatever the contemporary "modern" dialect may be. It *always* takes the direction from the first of these to the second, for it must point to the Word that goes *forth* from God and goes *to* man. But it never claims the first without the second, and certainly not the second without the first, for it must always contain both. Practical theology is studied in order to seek and to find, to learn and to practice, this speech that is essential to the proclamation of the community in preaching and teaching, in worship and evangelization. For these reasons practical theology must also be studied as long as one lives.

In conclusion, one marginal comment is needed about the entire theme of study. All those on the right or on the left, whose spirits are all too cheerful and naïve, may and should repeatedly discover anew in the study of theology that everything theological is somewhat more *complicated* than they would like it to be. But those spirits who are all too melancholic and hypercritical should discover and rediscover that everything here is also much more *simple* than they, with deeply furrowed brow, thought necessary to suppose.

Theological work is service. In general terms, service is a willing, working, and doing in which a person acts not according to his own purposes or plans but with a view to the purpose of another person and according to the need, disposition, and direction of others. It is an act whose freedom is limited and determined by the other's freedom, an act whose glory becomes increasingly greater to the extent that the doer is not concerned about his own glory but about the glory of the other. Such a serving act is the work of the theologian, whether this work is prayer or study or both simultaneously. Once again defined in general terms, it is *ministerium Verbi divini,* which means, literally, "a servant's attendance on the divine Word." The expression "attendance" may call to mind the fact that the New Testament concept of *Diakonos* originally meant "a waiter." The theologian must wait upon the high majesty of the divine Word, which is God himself as he speaks in his action. There is no better description of the freedom and honor of the theologian's action than the notable image in Psalm 123: "Behold, as the eyes of servants look to the hand of their master, as the eyes of a maid to the hand of her mistress, so our eyes look to the Lord our God, till he have mercy upon us." Theological work is a concentrated action by the very fact that it is also eccentrically oriented toward its *telos,* or goal. We must now attempt to understand it with respect to this inalienable and characteristic orientation.

In Calvin's famous classification of the ecclesiastical ministry the "deacon" occupies only the fourth and last place; what is allotted him is "only" to provide for the community's poor and sick. The "presbyter" precedes him and is responsible for the external conduct of the life of the community. He, in turn, is preceded by the "pastor," who is the preacher, instructor, and community parson. At the head of Calvin's ecclesiastical hierarchy, however, there is the "doctor," the teacher of the Church who, *ex officio*, interprets and explains the Scriptures. Obviously, he is, in particular, the theologian. Calvin certainly did not intend this classification to be as static as it appears or as it has frequently been understood and practiced. In any case, the *doctor ecclesiae* and the theologian, as the leading figures, will find it not only advisable but also necessary to become speedily, according to the Gospel, the last figure—the servant, waiter, and "deacon" for all the others. On the other hand, a fact also worthy of note is that the "waiting" of the martyr Stephen and of a certain Philip—those two "deacons" who are the only ones to be frequently mentioned in the Acts of the Apostles—seems to have consisted, according to the presentation of Luke, in searching and interpreting the Scriptures (Acts 6–8).

If, then, theological work is a special service which may technically precede all others, it cannot, all the same, wish to be more than service or ministry. It is not fit for anything unless it also, though in quite a special way, is provision for the poor and sick in the community. The corresponding truth is that Christian ministry of this practical type would also not be possible without a minimum of serious theological work.

To delimit our theme, the first thing to be said about the character of theological work as service is that it cannot be pursued for its own sake, in the manner of "art for art's sake." Whoever is seriously engaged in theological work knows that such a temptation lurks in many corners. Theology, especially in its form as dogmatics, is a uniquely fascinating science, since its beauty irresistibly elicits the display of intellectual architectonics. As inquiry into both the bright and the dim, or dusky, figures and events of Church history, theology is at every point highly exciting, even from a purely secular point of view. And as exegesis, it is equally exciting because of the way in which it calls in equal measure for both minute attention and bold imagination.

Theology is an enterprise in whose performance one question can all too easily be forgotten: For what purpose? Of course, this question may and should be set aside for the moment. Study is impossible when a student supposes he has to know and impatiently ask along every step of the way: Why do I need just this or that thing? How shall I begin to put this to use? Of what value is this to me in the community and the world? How can I explain this to the public, especially to modern men? He who continually carries such questions about in his heart and upon his lips is a theological worker who can scarcely be taken seriously either in his prayer or in his study. He who never lets himself be totally involved, or at least seriously engaged, by theological problems as such, but who concerns himself with them only in order subsequently to elevate himself by means of ready-made and patent solutions, will definitely not be able to say anything proper to the people. Much less will he be able to say the *one* thing that is fitting. The one right thing will be said only after the theologian's first endeavor has been to make personal acquaintance with something that is relevant, right, and proper. And he had better not immediately thereafter glance furtively at this or that practical application. The theological beginner should concentrate on his study in its own right during his few years at the seminary or university, for these years will not return. It is no doubt unwise, if not dangerous, when, instead of such concentration, the beginner flings himself beforehand into all sorts of Christian activities and ruminates on them, or even stands with one foot already in an office of the Church, as is customary in certain countries.

Nevertheless, this admonition does not alter the fact that the service of God and the service of man are the meaning, horizon, and goal of theological work. This goal is no gnosis floating in mid-air and actually serving only the intellectual and aesthetic impulse of the theologian. It is neither a gnosis of a speculative and mythological kind like that of the major and minor heretics of the first centuries, nor a gnosis of a historical-critical kind like that which began to flourish in the eighteenth century as the sole true theological science and which today is preparing to celebrate, if appearances do not deceive, new triumphs. If the proclamation or adoration of strange gods lurks behind the first kind of gnosis, skepticism or atheism lurks behind the second. After his fashion, Franz Overbeck no doubt was right when he pursued the way of this modern gnosis to its end and became wholly disinterested in theology as service. Although a member of the faculty of theology, he wanted to be and to be called, no longer a theologian at all, but—as may be read on his tombstone—only a "professor of Church history."

If theological work is not to become sterile in all its disciplines, regardless of how splendidly it may develop at one point or another, it must always keep sight of the fact that its object, the Word of God, demands more than simply being perceived, contemplated, and meditated in this or that particular aspect. What is demanded of theological work is the service of this word and attendance upon it. This may not always be its primary goal, and often it is the most remote one, but it remains its ultimate and real goal.

As a further delimitation of our theme, a second remark must be made here. Since theology is called to serve, it must not rule. It must serve both God in his Word as the Lord of the world and of the community, and the man loved by God and addressed by God's Word. It may rule neither in relation to God nor in relation to men.

In our very first lecture we spoke of the modesty that befits theology. The ultimate basis of this modesty is the fact that theology is a service. Such modesty does not exclude but rather includes the fact that theological work may and should be done with calm self-assurance. Nowhere is it written that the congregation of theologians will have to join in the long line of worms which, according to a song in Haydn's *Creation,* can only creep along the ground. If theology is not ashamed of the Gospel, it does not need to excuse itself to anyone for its own existence. It does not need to justify its action before the community or the world, either by constructing philosophical foundations or by other apologetic or didactic devices. Precisely because of its character as service, theological work should be done with uplifted head or not at all! Nevertheless, no one can engage in theology for the sake of earning a first prize or of securing for himself the highest status. A theologian cannot conduct himself like one who pretends to know all or who tries to outshine all those in the community who are less thoroughly learned and informed about the Gospel. Theology cannot vaunt itself in comparison with the achievements of other learned and informed men, and least of all, in comparison with other theologians.

Since the Word of God lays claim to the service of the theologian, it does not allow him to gain control over it (and by no means does it command him to do so). In this respect, the theologian cannot present or conduct himself as the expert or superior authority in contrast to the fools *intra et extra muros ecclesiae.* It would be presumptuous to imagine that he might and could gain control over the Word and over the object of his science, for in that event the Word would cease to be the object of theology. The theologian's whole endeavor would then lose its object and become, consequently, meaningless.

Indeed it is also said of theologians: "Who hears you, hears me!" But this does not signify the founding of a "papacy of biblical scholars," as Adolf Schlatter once termed it. For the "you" to whom this was said by Jesus are certainly no triumphal little popes, not to speak of crowned or uncrowned popes, but people who at Jesus' invitation took the lowest places at his table. From this position they might, at his invitation, be moved somewhat further upward. Those who "know more" and are "justified" in their own eyes, when it comes to the Word, are precisely those who keep sight of the fact that this Word disposes over them and that they do not dispose over it. They have to serve it, and it does not have to serve them or help them toward the fulfillment of some claim to power, whether public or private—not even when the best intentions support it. They reckon with the possibility that quite suddenly some minor character in the community (the "little old lady" in the congregation, so well known to every pastor!) or perhaps some peculiar stranger and outsider might be better informed in a most important respect about the subject on which everything depends. Some such person might know more than they do, with all their science and all their disciplines, and they might find occasion to learn many things from him instead of tutoring him. In the meanwhile, they will do their best in prayer and study, with uplifted heads, as upright men who intend to take pleasure in their work for a moment. They are confident because what they do is permitted them as deacons, in the special freedom granted them and with the special honor due them as servants. Precisely *this* service, on which they have no more claim than any others, has been entrusted to them as the service belonging to their bit of theological science.

But what are the consequences if the sense of theological work is the *ministerium Verbi divini*, attendance on the divine Word? Let us keep one thing clearly before our eyes: just as God's work is his free work of grace, so is his Word spoken in this work his free Word of grace. It is free as his own Word, resounding by its own power and making itself be heard. No man, not even God's community or theology itself, can appropriate, imitate, or repeat this Word. The frequently quoted short table of contents to the Second Helvetic Confession of Faith, written by Heinrich Bullinger, does not suggest an identification when it states in the second section of the first paragraph: *Praedicatio verbi Dei est verbum Dei* (The preaching of the Word of God is the Word of God). According to the context, what it states is: "When the Word of God today . . . is declared (*annuntiatur*) in the Church, we believe that the Word of God itself (*ipsum Dei verbum*) is there declared and is heard by the faithful." In this unity which is known by faith, *the* Word which is spoken by God is one thing, and what the man says who declares this Word is another. There can be no question of a transubstantiation of the first into the second or of the second into the first. What may and must occur in the act of human proclamation is the *annuntiatio*, the declaration of God's Word. *Praedicatio*, or preaching, is a declaration chosen by the Word itself. In it the Word will be mirrored and echoed. In *general* terms, this is the precise sense of all Christian service, including the service of theology.

The *special* service of the attendance of theology on the Word of God must all the same be distinguished from other actions by which the community serves its Lord. The service of theology can be best described in the following way: with respect to preaching, teaching, and counseling, which are at least not directly its own concern, theology must pose the *question about truth*. Theology must aid these activities toward those clarifications which they need to attain, and which they can achieve when they pass an examination regarding their truthfulness. Theology, of course, has no power nor is it commissioned to activate the Word of God itself. But just the same, it is authorized and commissioned, as a secondary witness, to support the entire proclamation of the Church in its task of mirroring God's Word as exactly as possible and of echoing it as clearly as possible. This secondary testimony of the community will quite likely never, and under any circumstances, be so perfect that a confrontation with the question about truth would be superfluous or unnecessary.

For instance, in the life of the Christian community it can never be taken for granted that the community serves the Word of God by all its projects and institutions. The fact may be, instead, that the Word of God is being made to serve the community and its projects and institutions. Theology must continually remind the community in every possible way of this danger.

Furthermore, it cannot be taken for granted that the connection of Church proclamation to the witness of the Old and New Testaments is and remains not only acknowledged, but also practically effective. Theology must constantly remind the community of this connection and encourage it to become free from all other entanglements.

Furthermore, in what the community does or does not do, says or does not say, it can all too easily under-

mine the fact that it has been called to proclaim to the
world *God*'s Word and not some other word which cir-
culates elsewhere in the world and repeatedly penetrates
into the community itself. The corresponding fact
that God's Word is directed to *man* can also, all too
easily, be weakened, obscured, or even denied. God's
Word engages man's attention as, in the last and decisive analysis, the free and divine Word of grace. Theology must illumine these matters from every possible
perspective.

The proclamation of God's Word in the community
can also sacrifice its center, or its contours as well, by
failing to understand and speak of this Word clearly
and expressly as the Word spoken by God in the history
of Israel and of Jesus Christ. Theology must come to
the aid of the community by speaking, on its part, intensely and comprehensively about this *concrete* Word.

When it proceeds properly, Church proclamation must
follow the direction from above to below, from the shining life of God into the shadowy substance of the individual and collective life of humanity. Theology must
demonstrate this movement in a manner exemplary
for Church proclamation, making this movement impressive and winning. This movement is the law and
freedom of the *intellectus fidei*.

Church proclamation can suffer at one point from
all too excessive many-sidedness and unhealthy over-
extension; at another point, from equally unhealthy one-
sidedness and narrowness in its subject matter. Here
it may suffer from liberal softening and distraction;
there, from confessionalistic and, perhaps also, bibli-
cistic or liturgical ossification and constriction. Against
one threat or the other, and as a rule against both
simultaneously, theology will admonish Church proclamation to concentration and openness. Church proclamation will under all circumstances be always more or

less strongly influenced by local, national, continental, or by social and racial traditions, and also by obvious prejudices, not to speak of the accidental or arbitrary aspects of situations which are determined by purely individual factors. In contrast to such influences, theology will have to stand guard over the purity of the Christian message and insist on the ecumenical, catholic, and universal sense and character of this message.

Wherever theological work is done, such clarifications will be inevitable along all these or similar lines. Since theology must serve the Word of God by its critical questions, acting without fear or favor, it will always stand in a certain salutary tension with the course and direction of Church existence. And the life and work of every church (whether a state church or a free church) will demonstrate clearly whether such clarifications are taking place in it and whether theological work is or is not also being done in it. Church life will show plainly whether a given church favors the service of theology or whether the people gathered in it, along with its bishops and other spokesmen, hold the opinion that they may dispense with theology. Existing all the while in a vitality and security which are only supposedly spiritual, they may think they can get along just as well, or perhaps even better, without theological work. In this latter case, Christianity and so-called culture might possibly come to the parting of the ways against which Schleiermacher warned so passionately. But this need not happen, and even if it did occur, it would not be the worst thing that could happen. What would be the worst thing, no doubt, is that the quest for truth in Christianity, without the ministering support of theology, would fall asleep on duty. As a result, the truth—which must be sought if it is to become known and familiar—would have to sever itself from Christianity. Theological work has a great responsibility in

the realm of the Church. The Church likewise has no
less a responsibility in its realm to engage in serious
theological work.

One concludirTg question remains; it cannot be more
than a question. Since theological work is service in the
community, indirectly it is also service in the *world* to
which the community is commissioned to preach the
Gospel. But is theological work, beyond this, also *direct*
service in the world? Should the clarifications which it
has helped achieve in the community also have significance, *mutatis mutandis,* for the general cultural life of
mankind (for instance, for the sense and procedure of
other human sciences)? Should it also be necessary to
art, for example, or to politics, or even to economics?
Should it have something to say to them and aid to offer
them? Such a thought can only be a question here,
since the answer can only be given, reasonably enough,
not by theology, but by those whom theology actually
helped or failed to help. The case *might* be that the
object with which theology is concerned could be experienced, at least as a problem, *extra muros ecclesiae* as
well, whether consciously, half-consciously, or unconsciously. Philosophy, for example, might be looked upon
as having at its best moments visualized the object of
theology from afar, though without having seriously
come to grips with it. The fact that beneath and beside
the many other things which occupy men's attention,
theological work is also somewhere attempted, could
give cause for thought, whether this fact is noted with
disapproval or with respect. It could *de facto* serve as
a reminder that something like the work and word of
God ought to be considered, quite apart from all that
men will, do, think, and know, in addition to and in
contrast with these human activities. God's work and
word might function there as a limit, foundation, and
goal, as a motivation and mitigation for all that.

Let us make the assumption (which is no doubt permissible) that in the environment of the community there exists a more or less precise awareness of the need for orientation, limitation, clarification—a need which adheres to all human activities, including the proudest and most autonomous sciences. The proclamation of the community, as it was carried out throughout the centuries, has certainly contributed to the definition of an insight into that need. Therefore, the existence of a theological faculty among other university faculties may well be a meaningful phenomenon both today and in the future. After all, ages ago, the university itself grew out of the theological faculty.

We must now surpass all that was said in the fourth series of these lectures about the performance of theological work in prayer, study, and service. A concluding word must be ventured to indicate the dominant principle, which is the sole source of the promise that theology may be a good work, pleasing to God and helpful to men. Unless this principle is valid and effective, theology will at no time or place ever become such a good work

Each of our three preceding series of lectures was concluded with the naming of a dominant principle. At the goal of the first series, the subject was the Spirit; at the goal of the second, faith; and at the goal of the third, hope. Each time, from different points of view, this principle was the one and indispensable condition of theological science. Theology can only recognize this condition as one *previously* granted it by its object, and it can only treat it the way that one treats a gift freely given. Although determined to make use of it, theology can only be grateful for this gift. In all this it knows very well that if this *conditio sine qua non* were not previously granted it, its work would remain cold, fruitless, dead, and bad, in spite of any perfection which it might perhaps possess in other respects. As we heard previously, the Spirit alone, faith alone, and hope alone really *count*.

Once more we look at the fundamental condition of theology from the special point of view of the preceding three lectures. This condition approaches theology from its object, must be received from this object, and must be actively fulfilled by this object's liberating power. We now venture the statement that theological work is a good work when it is permitted to be done in *love*. It is a good work *only* there (but nevertheless there with certainty) where it is resolutely done in love. Therefore, love alone counts. But love *really* counts. It builds up, as Paul consolingly wrote. In a later verse he adds that love never ends. Together with faith and hope (and as "the greatest of these"), it abides even when everything else passes away. But the same Paul also warned that knowledge as such, knowledge *in abstracto,* and theological effort and work in themselves do not build up but puff up and are arrogant. Later he adds that if he did not have love he would be only a noisy gong or a clanging cymbal, even as an apostle, and even if he were capable of the most adequate human speech, or even the speech of the angels. Without love he would be nothing at all, however capable he might be of speaking prophetically, knowing all mysteries, or attaining and enjoying all possible knowledge (I Cor. 8 and 13)! We will consider ourselves both admonished and comforted by this. Without love, theological work would be miserable polemics and a waste of words. The most serious prayer, the most thorough and extensive study, or the most zealous service could not alter this result. Theological work can only be undertaken, continued, and concluded by the reception and activation of the free gift of love. But as a *good* work it may and should be done in love.

Something further must now be said about this, to conclude not only this fourth series of lectures but also our whole *Evangelical Theology.*

How can we avoid being reminded by the word "love," first of all, of the Eros so highly praised in Plato's teaching? Love, as Eros, is, in general terms, the primordially powerful desire, urge, impulse, and endeavor by which a created being seeks his own self-assertion, satisfaction, realization, and fulfillment in his relation to something else. He strives to draw near to this other person or thing, to win it for himself, to take it to himself, and to make it his own as clearly and definitively as possible. And in a special sense, love, as *scientific* Eros, is the same desire in its intellectual form. It is the soaring movement by which human knowledge lets itself be borne toward its objects and hurries toward them in order to unite them with itself and itself with them, to bring them into its possession and power, and to enjoy them in this way.

Without scientific Eros there would be no theological work (and here we recollect what was said about study as such). Theological work is certainly also a human intellectual movement and, in its physical substratum, a human movement of the living person. Scientific, theological Eros has perpetually oscillated concerning the object which it should present to man for the sake of his self-assertion and self-fulfillment. That is to say, theological Eros can be directed either predominantly (and perhaps even exclusively) toward God or predominantly (and, once again, perhaps even exclusively) toward man.

The knowing subject can be interested either primarily in God or primarily in man. Its wish can be to comprehend, possess, enjoy, and, in this sense, to know either God above all or man above all. In the theology of antiquity and of the Middle Ages, scientific Eros expressed itself more in the first and theocentric direction. Conversely, in the more recent theology determined by Descartes, it tended more in the second and anthropocentric direction. To the extent that this object in fact has to do with both God and man, both emphases were not without foundation in the true object of theology. However, this very object never really permitted such oscillation, wavering, or separation between God and man as is characteristic of the history of scientific theological Eros. Moreover, another element intrinsic to scientific

Eros also does not arise from the object of theology. Whatever theologian allows himself to be ruled and motivated by Eros has a very remarkable capacity for wandering—yesterday he may have stood in the fields of idealism, positivism, or existentialism; today (probably for the sake of change) he may be in the domain of the Old and New Testaments; and tomorrow, as far as anyone knows, just as easily he may be found in the realms of anthroposophism, astrology, or spiritism. Are there any limits to what subject might be "interesting" or what "cause" urgent?

When scientific Eros evolves in the field of theology, it characteristically and continually confuses and exchanges the object of theology with other objects. So far as Eros is the motive of theological work, God will not be loved and known for God's sake, nor man for man's sake. This situation can only be explained by the nature of Eros: every attempt to love and know God and man is made in the quite conscious and deepest interests of the theologian himself, in the self-love of the one who produces this theology.

Let us not delude ourselves about the fact that this love will constantly be present wherever theological work is done! As surely as those who do this work are creatures of flesh and blood, so surely will they be affected by this love that, for its own purposes, needs and desires both divinity and humanity. Therefore, let us not suppose that we can or may deny that this type of love has its characteristic worth, power, and significance within the human situation. Eros forms, let us say, an outstanding phenomenon of man's spiritual life. Truly, nothing of small weight is involved when men believe it to be both necessary and desirous for them to love and know God *or* man or God *and* man in their *own* interest.

But one thing cannot be granted under any circumstances: that love of this kind would be identical with the love which makes theological labor a good work and without which this labor could certainly not become and remain good. To say that Eros was poured into our hearts by the Holy Spirit would obviously be possible only for someone blind or impertinent enough to ignore consistently all that Paul and the New Testament meant and expressed with these and similar words. Only such a person could say that Eros "builds up," that it "never ends," and that nothing is able to separate us from it (at the very least, our death will certainly do that!). Only so could it be named in the same breath with faith and hope (quite apart from the poor taste of such combinations) or explained together with them as the substance that remains after the great and general passing away of everything else.

It is undoubtedly no mere accident that the substantive "Eros" and its corresponding verb do not appear at all in the writings of Paul and the rest of the New Testament. The word for "love" in the New Testament is Agape. And from every context in which it appears the conclusion is obvious that it signifies a movement which runs almost exactly in the opposite direction from that of Eros. Love in the sense of Agape is admittedly also the total seeking of another, and this is the one thing that it has in common with love as Eros. In Agape, however, the one who loves never understands the origin of his search as a demand inherent within himself, but always as an entirely new freedom for the other one, a freedom which was simply bestowed on him and consequently was originally alien to him. On his own, he never should or would have loved this other one at all. But he *may* do this, and since he may do it, he *does* do it. Because he is free for this *other*, he loves *him*. In this way he loves concentratedly, not haphazardly, ramblingly, or distractedly. And because he is free for him, he does not seek him as though he needed him for himself as a means to his self-assertion and self-fulfillment. The one who loves, seeks the other only for his own sake. He does not want to win and possess him for himself in order to enjoy him and his own power over him. He never trespasses on the freedom of the other, but by respecting the other's freedom, he simply remains quite free for him. He loves him gratis. That is to say, he desires nothing from him, and he does not wish to be rewarded by him. All he desires is to exist for him, to offer himself to him, and finally to give himself to him. He desires to be permitted to love him simply in the way that this ability has been granted to himself. If love, in the sense of Agape, is no doubt also a seeking, it is nevertheless not an interested, but a sovereign seeking of the other one. "Giving is more blessed than receiving." This seeking is sovereign precisely because it is directed and oriented not to the sovereignty of the one who loves but to the sovereignty of the beloved one. To speak once more with Paul, love in the sense of Agape is patient and kind, not jealous or boastful, not arrogant or rude, not insisting on its own way. It rejoices in the truth, bears, believes, hopes, and endures all things. Agape is related to Eros, as Mozart to Beethoven. How could they possibly be confused? Agape is an altogether positive striving toward the other, quite distinct from all self-righteousness and intellectual superiority, as well as from all strife.

At this point the question may remain undecided whether it would not also be beneficial for the other sciences if the ruling motive of their procedure was Agape rather than Eros. For theological work the dominant position of love is a vital and unalterable necessity. Indeed, theological work also displays that interest of the perceiving human subject and that sweeping movement in which it allows itself to be borne and

hurried toward the object to be known. These elements
of Eros will not be simply suppressed or eliminated in
it. For theological work, however, Eros can only be the
serving, not the ruling, motive. The erotic wish and
desire to gain possession of the object can have in theological work only the significance of a first and inevitable
beginning in the direction toward its object. Wish and
desire will form only an attempt; they will be ready to
step back cheerfully before the object of their venture.
They yield gladly when their object makes an altogether
different attempt, not only to purify and to control them,
but also to transform them according to its nature and
to integrate them into itself. In theological work there
must be an end to the dominion of Eros, even if not an
end to scientific Eros as such. The love which has dominion in this work can only be the Agape which is
activated as a new and strange factor in theological
work. This Agape is introduced by the very object
which is to be known in it, in contrast to the knowing
human subject and his Eros.

The object of theological work is, in fact, a unity. This
unity forbids not only rambling and distraction in every
possible depth, height, and breadth, but also every inner
opposition. It forbids that dualism in which, as was so
often the case, theological work could waver back and
forth between friendship for God and friendship for
man, reacting now toward one and now toward the
other. The object of this work is the one true God and
the one true man. The true God exists not in his aseity
and independence but in his union with the one true
man. And the true man likewise exists not in his independence but in his union with the one true God. The
object of theology is, in fact, Jesus Christ. This means,
however, that it is the history of the fulfillment of the
covenant between God and man. In this history the
great God gave and offered himself in his own primal

freedom to be the God of small man; but, in this history, the small man also gave and offered himself, in the freedom given him by God for this act, to be the great God's man. This history took place uniquely, once for all, scorning all attempts to surpass it. The object of theological knowledge is this covenant event and, in it, the perfect love which unites man with God and God with man. In this love there is no fear. This perfect love drives out fear because in it God loved man for his own sake and man loved God for his own sake. What took place on both sides was not a need, wish, and desire but simply the freedom to exist for one another gratis. This was God's own primal freedom for man and at the same time man's freedom which was granted him by God. This was Agape, which descends from above, and by the power of this descent, simultaneously ascends from below. Agape is both movements in equal sovereignty, or, rather, this *single* movement.

If the object of theological knowledge is Jesus Christ and, in him, perfect love, then Agape alone can be the dominant and formative prototype and principle of theology. At this time and place, we may be sure that our knowledge will never become equal to Jesus Christ. In relation to him our knowledge will always be imperfect and inadequate because it will be obscured by every variety of the unrestrained and unconverted Eros that accompanies it. We are still in the state and pathway of the *theologia viatorum*, of the pilgrims who in every respect are *simul justi et peccatores*, simultaneously righteous and sinning. But this cannot mean that theological knowledge might withdraw from the dominion and formative power of perfect love, or that it might take its tiny steps along a path different from the one assigned it. Theological knowledge and theological posing and answering of the question about truth will, instead, only be properly done in the very measure that they render the life and dominion of perfect love visible *per speculum,* through a mirror, no matter how clouded this mirror may be. In its character as *opus operantis,* that is, with respect to the one who performs this act, theological knowledge will be a good work, pleasing to God and men and salutary for the Church and the world, to the extent that it is, remains, and repeatedly becomes free by renewed consideration of the *opus operatum Jesu Christi,* the work of Jesus Christ which is performed. This knowledge is good when it becomes free for *the* freedom with which God offered himself to man gratis and which he gave to man so that man might correspondingly give himself to God gratis. As *evangelical* theological knowledge, it cannot be won by any wishes, postulates, or requirements. It can be accomplished only by acknowledgment and confirmation of what is previously given it as its own prototype, i.e., the work of God: love in Jesus Christ. It is and remains subordinate and subsequent to that love; but it attempts to correspond to perfect love in spite of all imperfection. This orientation toward the perfect love is what may be somewhat dryly designated as the *objectivity* of theological work. In all its disciplines the same objectivity is required. When cultivated and pursued in this objectivity, theology is a modest, free, critical, and happy science, to recall once again those key words of our first lecture.

Will it really be this? Those who are active in this work cannot guarantee that it will be and is such a science. The situation is no different here than with the Holy Spirit, faith, or hope, none of which can be possessed, produced, or procured. The decisive presupposition of theological work is also its boundary. It is good that this should be so. For this means that those who are occupied with theology are compelled all along the line to look beyond themselves and their work in order properly to do what they do. The situation is no different with perfect love, which is the aspect under which we have attempted to look once again directly at the decisive presupposition of theology. In some sort of form and potency, Eros can be presupposed with every man. Agape, however, cannot be presupposed for *any* man. Only as a gift can it be received and set in action by any man, including any theologian at any time or place. It is "in Christ Jesus our Lord" (Rom. 8:39). It is where he is, works, and speaks. And since he is our sovereign Lord, what Luther said about the Word of God also holds true for Agape. It is "a passing thunderstorm" that bursts at one moment here and at another moment elsewhere. At all times and on all occasions, theological knowledge can take place and be accounted good in affinity to the gift and presence of that love. But something else also holds true of him in whom that love is real and true as both divine and human love. Whoever calls on his name will be saved. That is to say, whether or not the thunderstorm bursts, such a person may live and work with a *promise*. He is promised that perfect love is the heaven spread out over him, whether or not this love is momentarily clear or hidden from him. Protected and encouraged by the promise of this love, he may pray, study, and serve; and trusting in it, he may think, speak, and finally also die. Once a man knows where to seek and from where to expect the perfect love, he will never be frustrated in his attempts to turn himself to it and to receive from it an orientation which enlightens his small portion of knowledge. This love *abides* in the one in whom the covenant between God and man is fulfilled. It abides even when theologians come and go and even when things become brighter or darker in theology. It abides like the sun behind the clouds, which more precisely is and remains victoriously

above the clouds as "the golden sun."** To know about
the perfect love is in every case better than *not* to know
about it. It is better to know about this *conditio sine
qua non*, this indispensable condition, even if all that
can be done is to sigh for it. Simply to know about it
affords ample occasion to join in the praise of God, the
God of the covenant, the God who is love itself. It is
the very purpose of theological work, at any rate, to
know about this love and, therefore, to join in the praise
of God as expressed in the words of that familiar section
of the liturgy of the early Church, with which we may
now conclude:

> *Gloria Patri et Filio et Spiritui sancto*
> *Sicut erat in principio et (est) nunc et (erit) semper*
> *et in saecula saeculorum!*
> Glory be to the Father and to the Son and
> to the Holy Spirit
> As it was in the beginning, is now and ever shall be,
> world without end!

* "The Golden Sun" is the title of a hymn by Paul Gerhardt, 1666.